COMMUNICATION IN THE HUMAN SERVICES

A **SAGE** HUMAN SERVICES GUIDE **13**

SAGE HUMAN SERVICES GUIDES

a series of books edited by ARMAND LAUFFER and published in cooperation with the Continuing Education Program in the Human Services of the University of Michigan School of Social Work.

COMMUNICATION IN THE HUMAN SERVICES

A Guide to Therapeutic Journalism

Marcia S. JOSLYN-SCHERER

Published in cooperation with the Continuing Education Program in the Human Services of the University of Michigan School of Social work

 SAGE PUBLICATIONS   Beverly Hills   London

For information address:

SAGE Publications, Inc.
275 South Beverly Drive
Beverly Hills, California 90212

SAGE Publications Ltd
28 Banner Street
London EC1Y 8QE, England

Printed in the United States of America

Library of Congress Cataloging in Publication Data
Main entry under title:

Joslyn-Scherer, Marcia S.
    Communication in the human services.

    (Sage human services guides; v. 13)
    Bibliography: p.
    1. Journalism-Social aspects. I. Title.
PN4749.J66   302.2'3   79-28653
ISBN 0-8039-1418-0

FIRST PRINTING

CONTENTS

ABOUT THIS BOOK

Marcia Joslyn-Scherer's book continues in the tradition of the *Sage Human Service Guides*. Like each volume in the series, it introduces the reader to a specific practice tool that can be used in a variety of human service contexts. The journalist, the public relations officer, the school principal or hospital administrator, the mental health officer, the child welfare worker, and others will find many fresh ideas and how-to-do-it tips throughout the volume.

All volumes in this series are published cooperatively with the University of Michigan Continuing Education Program in the Human Services. Professor Armand Lauffer is series editor.

INTRODUCTION

Picture a wall. Put a mental sign on it that says, "Therapeutic Wall." On one side scatter a few *succumbers*, on the other an equal number of *copers*. Place on top of the wall a large number of *wall-sitters*—those people who are in the middle, betwixt and between, precariously waivering until they ultimately fall to one side or the other.

In the middle of this wall install a revolving door. Around this door and strategically located close to the wall, place some *wall-keepers*. The wall-keepers have many names: social workers, rehabilitation counselors, psychologists, physicians, therapists of all types. Their wall-keeping rules and regulations differ according to their label and training, but basically the wall-keepers try to do the following:

(1) Move the succumbers closer to the wall and, ideally, over to the side of the copers.
(2) Keep the copers from using the revolving door to return to wall-sitting or succumbing.
(3) Push the wall-sitters, by far the majority of people, through the door and over to the ranks of the coping. Then lock the door so these people can't turn back.

A therapeutic journalist is a new kind of wall-keeper. This person does not relieve or replace any other wall-keeper, but is an auxilliary useful in:

(1) Pulling and pushing the wall-sitters through the revolving door to the coping side of the wall.
(2) Using the coping styles of the copers to help the sitters without drawing the copers back toward the wall.
(3) Providing continuous support to the copers.
(4) Slowly and patiently putting the succumbers in motion to scale the wall.

The therapeutic journalist does all this with ideas, words, and thoughts translated from one person to another via media. The therapeutic journalist supports and reinforces the copers (educates them on alternatives, better ways, new resources), spends most of his or her time pushing and pulling the wall-sitters, and plants the seeds for change in the succumbers. The therapeutic journalist puts wall-sitters, copers, succumbers, and wall-keepers in a situation where they can exchange views and interact through media.

Now there are some who say there is no "Therapeutic Wall." They believe we are all basically the same and temporarily differ in our state of balance. But others, who seem to be in the fore right now, say there is a clear line or wall. They make this wall with diagnostic labels. They regulate movements with prescriptions and a mixed bag of therapeutic activities. A successful conqueror of the "Therapeutic Wall" receives a special commendation: discharge papers. This is supposed to help the person overcome the next and most important wall: that between deviancy and normalcy, the institution and the community, societal rejection and acceptance. The therapeutic journalist wall-keeps here too, as do the courts and the job market.

What is offered between the front and back covers of this book will provide you with tools, techniques, and resources that will be useful in your job as a wall-keeper or wall-razer. It is your guidebook. Feel free to mold its ideas to fit your interests and experiences.

Although there are many examples we can point to of existing therapeutic journalism efforts, there is no guiding philosophy, rationale, or purpose to tie these isolated efforts together. Once communication channels can be opened, we can systematically do away with debilitating miscommunications and gaps in communication that all too frequently build and strengthen walls.

This book will take some social science principles, some theories from communication, some trends in health and journalism, mix them all up and produce a concept we will call therapeutic journalism. You will find that the creation of a therapeutic journalist is a developmental task. Because this holds true for my evolution as a therapeutic journalist, I have many people to thank who have over the years questioned, supported, and consoled me at the right times. Many thanks to:

Special people. Jay, Mom, and the rest of my family; Aristides Penetrante; Stanley Platman; and *TODAY's* contributors and all the mental health clients in Erie County, New York.

Special Agencies. The Mental Health Association of Erie County; Buffalo Psychiatric Center; the Erie County Department of Mental Health; the United Way of Buffalo and Erie County; the Alcohol, Drug Abuse, and Mental Health Administration; the New York State Office of Mental Health; the Mental Health Materials Center; Western New York Offset Press; Crisis Services; and Goodwill Industries.

Colleagues, mentors, and friends. Robert Rossberg, Marceline Jaques, Joseph Steger, Robert Grantham, Maxwell McCombs, and Frank Baker. Salutations to Tom, Jean, Liz, and Katy; Dick, Diane, and Rachael; Mike and Becky; John, Ellie, and Michelle; Pat; David, Linda, and Teddy; Jeanne; Marie; Ann.

Contributors. Martin Pauley for the photographs; State University College at Buffalo for the graphic artwork; Bette, Connie, Donna, and Arlene for their patience and typing skills. Thanks especially to Sara Miller McCune and Armand Lauffer for their support, ideas, and advice.

Part I

DEVELOPING THE CONCEPT

1

HELP COMES VIA TABLOID

The reader's orientation to helping with therapeutic journalism is the focus of attention in Chapter 1. The ingredients of therapeutic journalistic efforts are outlined in order to prepare the reader for the materials that follow.

IN 1973 I HAD IN MY POSSESsion a bachelor's degree in journalism, a desire to be of help to people, and a particular interest in the dynamics of mental health clients. To satisfy the desire and the interest, I became a volunteer in a community mental health center in western New York. Initially, I was offered the position of volunteer editor of the center's newspaper. In order to accomplish this task successfully, I needed to learn how that system operated, to get to know many clients, and to learn about the relevant resources in the community.

I noticed that the community emphasis for mental health clients was a relatively recent one, and that some people who had emotional or mental problems preferred going to private or general hospitals for their care. This type of person usually had a mild case of depression or a life-style upset. The hospitals for the most part had highly qualified staffs, and their patients got excellent if not the best care.

I also met some people with very severe emotional and mental disabilities. Many of them were unable to function independently. Such people were sent to the state hospital, where they associated with and modeled peers no better off than they, if not worse, and probably under the care of a foreign-trained physician who might or might not be able to understand the communication and cultural ramifications of their problems.

I also noticed that some mental health clients were called "involuntary" clients or patients. This word was unfamiliar to me. In fact, we do not talk about forced health care, only forced mental health care.

Finally, I realized that if all of the mental health clients were to be helped with all their varying needs and degrees of deviancy and suffering, we needed the support of a wide variety of other services. There *was* a variety of resources in 1973 in Erie County, but also communication gaps and voids. While the usual complement of hospitals, day-care programs, transitional living facilities, counseling services, and social clubs was available, there was no economically effective method of providing clients with practical hints on how to use the services and resources available. There was, in addition, no readily identifiable forum for clients to share with others their successes, concerns, discoveries, and comments about their experiences. There were gaps in the outlying rural areas: People were being dispersed further and further outward as one by one by one they were being discharged from the hospitals and sent, often grossly unprepared, into the community. No acknowledged resource attempted to deal with the stigma and community rejection these returning people had to face. In 1973 the community had already started to rebel against "the insurgence of crazy people into their neighborhoods."

As a recent college graduate, I was still able to conjure up some of the theories and models I had been inundated with for four years. I remembered one in particular where social systems were connected to a person by information and the person was connected to the social systems by behavior. The behavior of the person determined the information from the social system and the information from the social system served to regulate the person's behavior. What was missing in this simple scheme was mutuality of understanding; the desire of one to help meet the needs of the other; a communication interchange that mediated, buffered, supported, and eased movement. There was too much that could go wrong in this cold exchange of behavior for information and vice versa.

The need for a mediator between mental health client, service facility, and community was evident. Such a mediating resource, were it available and used, might bridge the gaps between therapeutic care and client self-reliance. It could provide a file of how-to-do-it guides accessible to clients on demand without requiring a professional go-between, and it would be a source of encouragement. It would provide models of behavior and provide a source of identification with the community, and be a comprehensive resource for people with a myriad of needs.

Clients and helpers needed information, and so did the community in order to willingly accept those with deviancy and disabilities. Each had to be made aware of the needs of the others so that a matching and integration could be achieved.

Being a journalist, a newspaper format came to mind. I chose this for several reasons. The format is "normal" in the sense that special-interest publications are an accepted phenomenon and can serve large segments of the population. A newspaper is economical to produce and distribute. It is familiar to almost everyone, is flexible in content, and can be readily monitored for accuracy, helpfulness, and clarity.

I put together a proposal for my publication and submitted it to the director of the community mental health center where I was volunteering. He liked it and circulated it to a variety of local institution, agency, and association heaɔ for support and feedback. The Mental Health Association of Erie County (a citizens' association advocating for the legal, therapeutic, and community needs of mental health clients) thought this would fit nicely into their program package. This association appointed me editor of a client-oriented publication to be designed according to what I had proposed.

"*TODAY*... YOUR MENTAL HEALTH IN YOUR COMMUNITY" started in 1974 and became the archetype of the therapeutic journalism concept, it and this author had developed together. *TODAY* is a free monthly publication with a circulation of approximately 3,600. Its support comes from United Way and the state and county departments of mental health. The publisher is the Mental Health Association of Erie County. *TODAY*'s readers are mental health clients, mental health and related-area professionals and paraprofessionals, and interested community representatives and residents. The cost of producing *TODAY* as a tabloid newspaper is roughly $600 per month. This figure includes printing costs, supplies, and miscellaneous staff and secretarial help. It includes mailing costs at a bulk rate and mileage for distribution to local facilities. It does not include editorial staff costs.

TODAY features a wide variety of services and resources that can be used to achieve satisfying and independent, yet interdependent, community living. Believing that open communication may lead to understanding and respect, *TODAY* publishes articles by local professionals, paraprofessionals, community people, and mental health clients. Its features on self-help, self-care, home care, money managing, legal rights, and job tips are all geared to serving the comprehensive needs of the whole person.

Community events and activities are publicized with special emphasis on those accessible to people with limited money and transportation. A goal of *TODAY* is to provide easier movement from mental health facility to the community and, if necessary, vice versa. Hence, resource identification in both of these areas is a prime focus. Since *TODAY*'s features are varied in terms of subject matter, depth, scope, and level of difficulty, it hopefully provides something of interest to every reader.[1]

TODAY immediately drew support and commendation. Soon the New York State Office of Mental Health began giving it special attention and advocated its duplication and replication in other New York counties. Then the Alcohol, Drug Abuse, and Mental Health Administration of the U.S. Department of Health, Education and Welfare published an article on the *TODAY* concept (Joslyn, 1976) and promoted the idea nationally. The paper also began winning some awards for community service and for journalistic quality and innovativeness.

Let's hold it for a minute. Right about now you might be saying to yourself: "One person's success does not guarantee that of another. Is this a *show and tell* kind of book where I'm supposed to 'observe and model' you? Even if I do like your ideas, can I tailor-make them to work for me?" The answer to each of these questions is *yes*. This is in part a show and tell book. I'll be sharing my experiences with you. It *is* something you can pull off, and it is something that you'll be able to do well given the necessary information and a little bit of experience. But before we delve into therapeutic journalism any further, I ought to share a few of my biases with you. Perhaps a quote from John Dewey concisely sums up most of my biases and the message of all that follows:

"There is more than a verbal tie between the words common, community, and communication" (1916: 5). If, after reading all the words to come, nothing more than this strikes home, you and the book will still have met with considerable success.

A clear view of where this guide fits into Dewey's triad depends on a concept of communication that strives to bring together people and resources—resources that are often available in the people's own communities or communal units. This is not a new goal of journalism, for this profession has since its inception informed, educated, enlightened, and entertained its readers with information about what is around them. What is new is the use of information about the community, similar others, and the self to aid in the promotion of physical and mental health, community adjustment and satisfaction, and self-understanding and acceptance. Journalism is being *therapeutic* when (1) it addresses a particular group with special needs (such as the aging, mental health clients, diabetics, the wheelchair-bound, and those people in any respect disadvantaged; (2) communicates sharing, belonging, and support; and (3) provides information on self-help, mutual aid, and resource utilization (resources of self, other, and community).

The therapeutic journalist looks at a group of people who have something in common, advocates a more advantageous use of the community by these people, and communicates ideas, tips, and techniques which the readers can use for self-enhancement. This can be done in any community and for any special-interest group.

A therapeutic journalistic endeavor is then quite an awesome responsibility to undertake. Because anyone attempting such a feat should have a solid background in people and community dynamics as well as in publication production, this book has been organized to take you through a sequence of developmental steps designed to develop you as both a communication and helping agent.

I've written this book with three audiences in mind, each of whom requires a somewhat different introduction: (1) the generic journalist, (2) the helper and therapist, and (3) the (mental) health communicator. The journalist, trained in communication through the media of television, newsprint, radio, and magazines may require more substance in understanding and helping the different kinds of people who live in our communities. The helper (the social worker, the rehabilitation counselor, the ex-client or patient turned [para]professional and advocate), on the other hand, requires a discussion of journalism tenets, techniques, and media. The (mental) health communicator (the hospital newsletter editor, the small agency public relations person, the writer of county health department brochures and news releases), already in possession of many therapeutic journalism skills, really only needs to be given an orientation to this book's interpretation of therapeutic journalism.

In these pages an attempt has been made to meet the needs of all three audiences—to give each some of the knowledge base of the others. Therefore, some sections may seem like "overkill" to the media-minded whereas other sections will include material familiar to the helping-oriented. The reader's indulgence is thus requested for portions that appear basic or redundant.

The journalist, helper, and (mental) health communicator will all receive new information in Chapter 2, where a unique view will be presented of journalism's impact on people and the community.

Certainly the journalist is an expert on the community. He or she must be in order to report on its events, activities, and resources. The helper, too, must know the community and its agencies in order to helpfully link client with resource. For purposes of therapeutic journalism the community will be considered a *system* with many subsystems operating within it: for example, it includes a subsystem of mental health clients which is made up of subsystems of individuals. The linking factor is communication. As will be seen in Chapter 3, communication makes possible channels among all other systems and subsystems.

In Chapter 4 the foundation is laid for therapeutic journalism. Not an entirely new concept, therapeutic journalism has for years used the media of newspapers, newsletters, or broadcasts to address particular special-interest groups (mental health clients, the aging, paraplegics, diabetics). It has adopted the role of "consumer advocate" and does a good job of keeping the community-based or -bound reader informed and aware of pertinent legislation, financial matters, community resources and activities, as well as providing tips on self-help and health maintenance. Group or communal solidarity is often an aim of therapeutic journalism, and it helps to achieve this through mutual aid features, information-sharing, and advisement. By using the time- and cost-efficient means of journalism, therapeutic media efforts can quickly meet the needs of a wide audience.

Therapeutic journalism efforts have a variety of uses. Although they may be primarily client- or patient-oriented, many have the objective of facilitating communication among (para)professionals, community representatives and residents, and the clients and patients. Hopefully, through "hearing" one another's point of view, better understanding will ensue.

As for the client or patient focus, many people undergoing health or mental health care are now widely dispersed around the community and no longer have the benefit of a ward's TV lounge or a small institutional community to assure their meeting with similar others. People in outlying rural areas present special problems. By being in the community at large and having to fend for themselves, they need quality information in quantity. Features centered on resource identification and utilization are becoming increasingly valuable in community survival.

Concomitant with the push toward institution-emptying (known in the field as the "deinstitutionalization" movement) and community placement is the consumer movement. Consumers of health and mental services are demanding more quality assurance in treatment programs, more humanizing care, and equal participation, or at least consultation, in their treatment regimes. Media offer the most viable, efficient, and economical means of regular contact for people who want to keep abreast of changes in the health and mental health areas, who want to keep informed of ways to self-assert and self-advocate, who want to learn self-care techniques for health and mental health maintenance and illness prevention, and who want to share and compare new ideas and approaches to healing through helping.

Therapeutic publications are rare. The recent report of the President's Commission on Mental Health made no mention of therapeutic publications in its recommendations. A 1977 publication of the National Institutes of Health on health education gave therapeutic journalism no better publicity (Marshall, 1977).

This dignified unobtrusiveness of therapeutic media has made them in some respects invisible. Certainly this makes for even greater room for the creative therapeutic journalist to experiment and gain unique recognition. However, the newness and unassertiveness do not make for a large pool of models to emulate and to measure against.

The sufficiently creative person may be willing to take the risks. As a matter of fact, taking "the road less traveled by" seems to be the current fashion. We have a movement now toward "self-publishing." Creative entrepreneurs are starting all kinds of specialized, small publications to fill the voids created by our "electronic media massage," as Marshall McLuhan, mass media critic, would call it. The therapeutic publication logically follows.

Besides offering the journalist a creative outlet, therapeutic publications allow the producer to be his or her own boss, provide the editor a chance to help the community, and give the writer a chance to help many people find a new or more positive group- or self-identity as reentering participants in a broader community life. The rewards are fantastic. The only one, in fact, that is least likely to find an outlet is the monetary or financial one. This is an unfortunate fact of life of the helping professions.

Regardless of whether the reader of this book identifies with the journalist group primarily, or the helper group, each has his or her own special talents to offer therapeutic journalism. As has been said, the journalists will be provided with background information of pertinent therapeutic dynamics. For the helpers who need some advice on journalistic principles and techniques, three chapters have been devoted to imparting knowledge and skills in this area: Chapter 2, is of a theoretical nature. It basically defines journalism and attempts to answer the question, "Why should journalism enter the therapeutic arena?" Chapters 5 and 6 are devoted to the practical subjects of tabloid production and distribution, ideas for attracting funding sources (or how to get someone to sponsor *your* therapeutic journalism effort), tips on establishing a contributor pool, ways to get the publications to where the people are, and so on.

Chapter 7 discusses what can be done and is being done around the country in the spirit of therapeutic publications. Publication examples are given, and alternative ideas are drawn from related efforts in radio, television, and the general press. Feel free to use these examples and build on and expand upon these ideas for your own purposes.

In Chapter 8 the evaluation of therapeutic journalism efforts is discussed. Theoretical concepts are complemented with examples of surveys. The forms used in the surveys presented are included in the Appendices for your use.

The final chapter provides a summary for the reader of the many ideas presented previously. It is an attempt to piece everything together into a meaningful whole.

Before moving onward, let me make one recommendation. Because each chapter covers many topics under its broad heading, read this book thoroughly and in order—even though sections may seem at first glance to be "old hat." The exercises I've included for your use should also be completed in order. The formulation of a comprehensive concept is a developmental task, and some congruity may be lost through the omission of paragraphs, pages, or exercises.

Finally, concepts such as *common, community,* and *communication* have been discussed without first defining them. The meanings of these terms for our purposes are unique and somewhat dependent upon one another. You will have a much better understanding of these concepts once a few chapters have been read. The definitions are, therefore, left to evolution.

Let us progress.

So Far:

(1) We need to think in terms of people with *common* needs and interests who are either in the *community* or being prepared for *community* reentry and who can benefit in many respects from an exchange of information (*through communication*) that involves diverse people, resources, and aspects of living.

(2) Therapeutic publications are the tools we can choose to accomplish the above. The development of the therapeutic publication concept evolves as shown below.

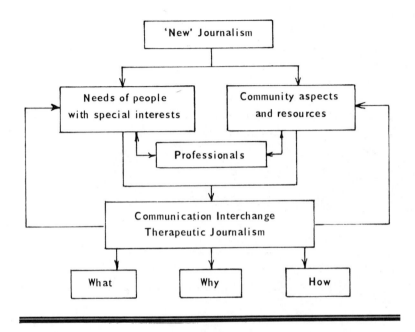

N O T E

1. To see for yourself what *TODAY* is like, you may receive a complimentary copy or "subscription" by writing to the address below:

> TODAY
> Mental Health Association of
>   Erie County, Inc.
> 1237 Delaware Avenue
> Buffalo, New York 14209

Tell them I sent you.

R E F E R E N C E S

BERTALANAFFY, L. von (1968) General Systems Theory. New York: George Braziller.
DEWEY, J. (1916) Democracy and Education. New York: Macmillan.

JOSLYN, M. S. (1976) "A new kind of client paper." Washington, DC: Alcohol, Drug Abuse and Mental Health Administration.

McLUHAN, M. (1966) Understanding Media: The Extensions of Man. New York: McGraw-Hill.

MARSHALL, C. L. (1977) Toward an Educated Health Consumer: Mass Communication and Quality in Medical Care. Washington, DC: U.S. Department of Health, Education, and Welfare (DHEW Publication No. (NIH) 77-881). Fogarty International Center Series on the Teaching of Preventive Medicine, Volume 7.

2

ADJUNCT THERAPIST

A Renewed Role for Journalism

Journalism's movement toward specialization is traced. Specialization as a development provides media options to readers and gives journalists room to experiment. As many people share common communication needs in special-interest areas, communication experts will find they can help and support people through the specialization in therapeutic journalism.

RECENTLY, I ATTENDED THE first meeting of an advisory committee for a community college's journalism technology program. The most striking feature of the meeting was its emphasis on the journalist as one who works in the community, and for the community, as a promoter of communication interchange among people, activities, programs, and events. We focused on the role of the journalist as an editor of church newsletters, community weekly newspapers, or agency and in-house publications. The goal was *not* to produce New York *Times* reporters or moguls of the mass media, but to educate and train good moderators of the matters of the community.

Perhaps this college has left the indoctrination and preparation for the sophisticated world of the "big-time" media up to the four-year journalism programs to instill. But there is another hypothesis; one that seems more in line with present media trends. That is: With the current movement toward the specialized press, the small press, the "New Journalism," there is a great need for people who can be trained quickly to communicate with special-interest groups and to interpret group interests and those of the "outside" world to one another.

The specialized media movement grew out of disillusionment and disenchantment with the general media which, some say, by trying to provide something for everyone, appealed to the special interests of no one. With leisure time—and money— becoming more common commodities, many people began to indulge in such activities as skiing, golfing, hunting, traveling, and boating. Each activity was seen as deserving of its own features to keep its enthusiasts abreast of new developments. As we began to experience an information explosion concurrent with a technological revolution, weeklies specializing in nothing but news and new developments began to gain territory over such staples as *Life* and *Look*. In the 1960s the "New Journalism" movement brought a myriad of out-of-the-norm pioneer publishing efforts to newsstands. Called "alternative" or "underground" papers, these efforts were another form of specialization.

The rapid growth of technology had the effect of making specialists out of everyone. The day of the true generalist was over when information could no longer be absorbed as fast as it was being created. Today, each specialty within each profession has at least a half-dozen journals devoted to items within its sphere of control. Concomitantly, we also see the resurgence of generalists within specializations. We have the generic journalist who can ideally fit in anywhere with any medium of public communication. We have the generic counselor or therapist who arranges comprehensive care and treatment for the "whole" person.

> **Point:**
> Health and mental health care are currently focused on the coordination of specialized services while journalism is moving away from generalization and toward quality specialization. Therapeutic journalism, a journalistic specialty, can be a major contributor to the coordination of services for a particular special-interest group.

Those of us in journalism, generic or not, should be pleased with the appearance of any new medium of public communication as more and more jobs have been created to fill the information gaps of our special-interest-segmented public. Yet journalists are in trouble. Jane Pauley of the Today Show on NBC, recently reported that there are now more students enrolled in journalism programs than there are total existing jobs in journalism. The media veterans will not turn over their desks, and newsroom mechanization has everyone running scared. So where will all the students go?

Many are starting their own publications, are buying small community weeklies or radio stations in remote regions of the country, or are trying to make a living through free-lancing. Their energy and enthusiasm are admirable. But there are limits to how much these markets can absorb. Another sad state of affairs is an apparent decline of interest in the daily newspaper. An Associated Press report of Friday, October 13, 1978 out of Cleveland reported on a survey of the news habits of Americans. The survey was conducted by Dr. John P. Robinson, director of the Communications Research Center at Cleveland State University. Dr. Robinson's results showed that newspaper readership is declining while a reliance on television news reports has grown somewhat in the last twelve years. The article stated, "The number of newspaper readers had dropped 11 percent from those who had read a paper in a similar survey done in 1965-66. There was an increase of 6 percent in those watching television news."

Will television put those of us who rely on ink and paper out of business?

Before you answer, consider that there is more to the story. It seems older persons make the most use of newspapers, but they are also more apt to watch television news than people in other age groups. Newspaper readers are characterized by higher ages, incomes, and educational attainment. As for the age difference, Dr. Robinson said, "Rather than being a generation turned off by newspapers, the under 30's appear to be a generation turned off by news."

Turned off by news? Perhaps there is another explanation for Dr. Robinson's statement. Our youthful adults may be trying to give us a message that says, for them, many items the media choose to highlight are irrelevant, redundant, or dull. This message may be especially significant when we consider that our youthful adults are often our most reliable advocates for and activators of change.

For a potential solution to this dilemma we must once again turn to the specialized media. We know youthful adults do have an interest in some media—professional journals, weekly news magazines, such publications as fashion, sport, and hobby magazines—and certainly favorite radio and television programs. They are not turned off to news per se, just certain kinds of news, just as they are turned on by certain topics and subject areas.

Marshall McLuhan gives a reason in his book, *Understanding Media: The Extensions of Man* (1966) for the possible decline of interest in the daily news. By trying to keep all of our citizens informed equally and simultaneously, we have diffused our knowledge bases. Everyone now knows a little about medical techniques, a little about legal procedures, something about the principles of aerodynamics. We have "amateur practitioners" in a large variety of areas. There are no longer any "sacred grounds" as far as the media are concerned.

By overwhelming people with bits and pieces of everything under the sun, we are bound to have readers—out of sheer desperation—tuning us out. It could be our youthful adults are reacting to an older generation's need to know something about everything through selective attention to the massive amounts of information available. To be selective, they go to the special-interest media. It is a sign of our times. If we are a specialized society, we must develop specialists to help and communicate with us.

Another critic of the established media is Cees Hamelink. In an article on *"An Alternative to News"* (1976), he says that when we are presented with incoherent, disjointed fragments of information—as in daily newspapers and television news broadcasts—we are treated as if we were great *depositories* of all that the media specialists care to unload on us. This puts us in a rather powerless position. We are, in fact, given only those information bits—however disorganized—that news sources and reporters care to share with us. As a force, then, for social cohesion the media are doing their jobs well. But as tools for creative change and growth, or even positive upheaval, they fall short. Hamelink's alternative is purposeful, holistic, systematic, and—most importantly—user-oriented media. In fact, they inject the reader with a sense of importance and self-mastery. Through a sharing of insights, people are divested of their depository, passive roles.

The rights of critics to criticize notwithstanding, the fact remains that *there is much virtue in both the established and the specialized media.* Each medium has its own file of quality credentials. In reality, the two styles are not that far apart.

Ethnic papers, patterned after the general press, often function therapeutically by keeping their readers in touch with one another and by keeping the focus on shared interests and common concerns. They are a major force in holding the ethnic group members together, and they help shape the group's and individual group member's identities. An example of this comes from New York City's *Jewish Daily Forward.* For generations a column entitled "A Bintel Brief" has included letters from immigrant readers who felt isolated, alone, and unable to cope with the complexities of a large metropolitan area with new life-styles. The columnists have answered as warm friends who provided understanding and the assurance that their concerns were legitimate ones. They also removed from the readers that sense of inadequacy that comes from having difficulties coping within the context of unfamiliar environments.

The Black press, too, has a help-one-another approach. It is common to see success stories featuring teachers, business-people, and technicians. These careers are within the reach of the readers and the successful peers are held up as role models. Ethnic or other special-interest-oriented radio and television programs similarly connect people with shared needs and interests.

When we really think about it, our daily papers and community weeklies serve much of these same functions when they feature the activities of familiar people in the midst of recognizable places and events. In fact, the general media derive their name from their ability to provide something for everyone. Columns and broadcasts featuring question and answer exchanges, helpful hints, and community resource identification all provide the audience with therapeutic opportunities for saying, learning, and doing.

So therapeutic journalism is not necessarily a *new* emphasis, but rather a *renewed* one. All media, general or specialized, have particular constituencies that require a certain special addressing through special features. What distinguishes one from the others is in the choice of what's covered and in what depth. Therapeutic journalism, then, is a shared and agreed-upon goal to help people with common needs and interests communicate on a variety of levels with others in possession of experience and information for the purpose of optimizing their community participation and societal contributions.

A look at the historical development of the press in America will further demonstrate how press specialization and therapeutic journalism are natural outgrowths of the general media.

Journalism in America began in the late 1600s in the area in and around Boston. At first the newspaper served a political function (advocating freedom, solidarity, and so on) and was, for the most part, the brain child of one man who served as writer, editor, layout man, and printer. Since people lived in colonies, the newspaper had a colonial or local focus; it was unconcerned with those folk in the next colony over. The Boston, New York, and Philadelphia colonies were self-absorbed. Rarely did they interact via the printed word.

As the pioneer spirit dispersed colonial residents, newspapers also changed. Many moved to where the most people were, the large cities. As the population and technology of the cities grew, the newspaper had to keep pace. The number of pages in the newspaper increased and so did its news. All this meant a larger staff to get "all the news to all the people all of the time." The one-man operation had broadened. Yet one man usually maintained control. He was the power behind the press, and he used his power to make his paper the best—and hopefully for him, the only—attractive source of news in town. This philosophy pitted publisher against publisher, editor against editor. A great sense of competition evolved. Some would try to buy up as many papers as they could to establish a media empire. (Today we are familiar with such sovereigns as Hearst, Newhouse, and Murdock.) As more and more power and wealth was sought, news was not valued for its own self but for its ability to sell papers. This brought disenchantment with the media on the part of some of the readers. A response has been a return to the small community papers. To fill the burgeoning interests of the public, the specialized press developed the needed expertise, broke away from the more established press, and made the decision to fly on its own. With radio and television added to this scenario, the media empires, which were so carefully constructed, are now fighting for their lives. They are trying to maintain indispensability in a time of changing interests.

Journalism from the word go was designed to keep people informed of those things important to their existence and the continued existence of their communities. Safety, freedom, and personal welfare were all concerns of the colonial newspaper. Some of that intent may have been lost when the media became big businesses. But it remains the purpose of journalism to *communicate* to people who share *in common* certain needs— those things which will enable them to lead satisfying personal, family or group, and *community* lives.

People have needs for certain kinds of information that can be met in part through journalistic efforts. As the needs or interests of readers change, so too does the focus of communication. Our specialized media movement is a response to the pressure put on the established media by communities and special-interest groups.

When people with common purposes and preferences express a desire for certain information, they expect that information to fit into their world view. The information must be coherent; it must be relevant. As in Hamelink's "alternative to news," information should be user-oriented and user-enhancing.

Information should also be salubrious, invigorating, and revitalizing. One particular aspect of living that pervades our entire being and our relationships to other people and the environment is our physical and mental health. When our health has gone awry, our view of everything in and around us is affected. If we are immobilized, interactions with others and the outer world are severely limited or possibly even nonexistent. When this happens, we can't communicate effectively and in some respects we may stagnate. Dr. Elisabeth Kubler-Ross (1969) has learned from the dying that a lack of certain kinds of communication can create a sense of abandonment, helplessness, and hopelessness. When communication is restored, so too is a sense of dignity, acceptance, and peace.

The plight of the mental health client provides an excellent example of the importance of communication to well-being. When the "emotionally and mentally deviant" were shut up in large institutions, it was in many cases for a life-time stay. New efforts to rehabilitate and reintegrate mental health clients into the mainstream of society have yielded some interesting findings about the effects of institutionalization. Putting people away and limiting the amount of stimulation they receive may cause a further disintegration of the personality. Still quite recently, an occasional patient would be found on some back ward who had been brought to a facility years ago because of alleged bizarre behavior when, in reality, that person had arrived normal, albeit a "different" normal. Such people might have come from another country, have been unable to speak English, and labeled "sick" because of repeated aborted communication attempts. They might or might not have arrived "perfectly sane," but when discovered years later as victims of faulty communication and nothing else, they had certainly *become* mentally ill and could now genuinely be classified as such.

There are different interpretations of this phenomenon. One is that people respond to what is expected of them in order to adapt to their new environment. "If I'm supposed to be sick, I guess I'd better act sick." Another interpretation, and the one favored here, is that a lack of stimulation from the environment can cause a person to deteriorate physically, mentally, and emotionally. Since communication is the key to any effective interaction, it is a vital force in keeping us well. People must be in a position to receive and offer information in order to maintain or enhance themselves. Degeneration is the alternative.

An example of communication voids many of us are personally familiar with is the rapid deterioration of older people upon the death of a spouse or upon being limited within the confines of a nursing home. A significant loss of communication-inter-action-stimulation plays a great role in these situations.

But what happens when an existing communication void tends toward satiation? A few things. To some it is filled with the first and only information available. This may become a significant concern if that information is what may be called "propaganda." For mental health clients who have been institutionalized for years and then "dumped" into communities, it has been filled with such a bombardment of miscellaneous stimuli that confusion and disorientation resulted. The void has been filled too fast with too much.

For some people who have yet to learn how to sort, categorize, and use information effectively, a communication void may be filled by anyone claiming to have what they lack: strength, power, and wisdom. The communicationally gifted often convince the confused to submit. Sadly, this recently resulted in a massive cult suicide/murder in Guyana.

Given that communication plays such an important role in people's lives, what can the journalist or journalism technician—as communication experts—do to enhance the positive effects of good communication? For one thing, they can jump on the bandwagons of the specialized media, news alternatives, and consumer movements by working to provide at least one special-interest group with information that strengthens, supports, and stimulates its members. When the target audience has common concerns and interests, and when the information provided to them helps to improve their health, self-image, and competencies, that information can be classified as *therapeutic*. When that information is provided via tabloid, magazine, and radio or TV show, we have not only new members of the specialized media but new members of the helping team. We have adjunct therapists whose tools of the trade are ink, paper, film, and microphone.

Therapeutic journalism has naturally evolved from journalism's history. By responding to trends in consumer affairs and health care, journalism is showing a willingness to grow and change; to take its best aspects and share them with others; to pool efforts with other disciplines to achieve a healthier citizenry.

Our improved lives depend upon an opening of communication channels among people at all levels of functioning community agencies of all sorts, and stimuli from all directions of the environment. A task ideal for the therapeutic journalist.

The economics of journalism also point toward a need for a new direction. With journalists flooding the job market, and with many old media friends fast fading away, it makes sense to branch out into areas that need our skills but have heretofore had to do without them. New endeavors in the broadcast and print media are not only needed by journalists but are desired by audiences.

As for the printed word as a means of therapeutic communication, it is still very much alive and viable in spite of publication perishability and a declining use of the daily newspaper. We have evidence of this in many successful special-interest publications. We have created a whole new role for ourselves when we use our talents with written language to bring *community* and those with something in *common* together via *communication*. When we develop expertise in these areas, and thereby make ourselves indispensable, we have grafted our own branch onto journalism's family tree.

To be a quality therapeutic journalist, then, one must know communication, a community, and a target group characterized by members with common needs and interests. Background in these areas is given in the next chapter.

ADJUNCT THERAPIST   37

So Far:

(1) People depend on communication for their health and well-being. Poor communication, communication voids, or mixed communications can be harmful and detrimental. Good communication can help us to be well and satisfied. Communication can be literally sickening or it can be therapeutic.

(2) A group of people who share common communication needs can be reached through media addressed to those needs.

(3) Those skilled in communication can create such therapeutic media.

(4) These specialized media are compatible with current journalism trends. As the needs and interests of readers change, so too do the media.

REFERENCES

HAMELINK, C. (1976) "An Alternative to News." Journal of Communication 26 (Autumn): 120-123.
KUBLER-ROSS, E. (1969) On Death and Dying. New York: Macmillan.
McLUHAN, M. (1966) Understanding Media: The Extensions of Man. New York: McGraw-Hill.

*"There is more than a verbal tie
between the words common,
community, and communication."*
—*John Dewey, 1916*

3

INTERACTION THROUGH
COMMUNICATION

The Conceptual Rationale for
Therapeutic Journalism

People need to be attached to others, the community, and to an even wider environment. Information and communication are what attach people to other systems. Communication is our major linking agent to people, resources, and all the systems we need for survival, health, and a sense of well-being.

REGARDLESS OF THEIR PARticular special interests, all people share the need for life-sustaining supplies, other people, and the community. As Figure 3.1 shows, all people are attached, at least partially, to their environment. The individual is in the center with links to other people and community resources. There are, according to Norris Hansell (1974), *seven essential attachments* that we need in order to feel healthy, happy, and complete: (1) supports necessary to existence (food, oxygen, and information), (2) the notion of identity, (3) connection with other persons, (4) connection to groups, (5) connection to a social role, (6) money and purchasing power, (7) a system of meaning.

Each Attachment is going to be discussed in light of its relevance for the therapeutic journalist. Because the first essential attachment is what makes all the others possible, and because it is the one you and I are most concerned with, the attachments are presented in reverse order so that the best is saved for last. We will end, therefore, at the beginning.

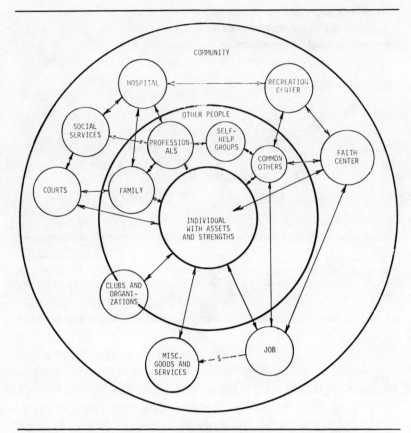

FIGURE 3.1: The Exchange and Interaction of Individuals, Other People, and the Community

WE NEED A PURPOSE IN LIFE

The *seventh attachment* is to a system of meaning, a purpose in life, an overall game plan in which we can actively participate. It is a way of connecting with our present while drawing on our past and projecting into the future. With this attachment we can overcome anything; without it we are totally lost as Frankl demonstrated in his account of the survivors of Nazi concentration camps (1962). Those who survived did so because they saw their situation within a broader context; they could look beyond their situation to a broader meaning and purpose in their lives. We are living in a time when the fallout from our technological and information explosions has left many of us disjointed from our past, without a clear direction, and without a concomitant sense of meaning. We feel trapped within a vacuum; lost in an aftermath of hopelessness, helplessness, and powerlessness.

Our time is one of flux. We see many concurrent movements that are in seeming disparity. People are attempting to rediscover a community and common others. They are striving to develop new patterns of communication interchange. But they are also experiencing communication voids, a lack of integration, a sense of meaninglessness. Just as we can see around us the popularity of self-help and mutual aid, we can also see the disintegration of the nuclear family, the closely knit neighborhood, the "we're-all-in-this-together" spirit of the small community. Familiar and traditional groupings are being broken apart as new bonds are being formed. While we develop the new, we are influenced by the old. We are experiencing all the anxieties associated with change.

These findings come from researchers at the University of Michigan (Kulka, 1978; Veroff, 1978). In two surveys designed to assess changes in feelings of well-being over two generations (the first survey was done in 1957, the second in 1976), the researchers found the anxiety engendered by our technological and information explosions. They found a need for the individual to be in control, not controlled. They found a lack of community integration, communication interchange; a void that has been demonstrated by higher anxiety levels, a sense of isolation, incompleteness. The researchers found a turning inward for personal happiness, a turning outward for the source of personal difficulty. People tend to blame the environment, others, and poor communication and interaction for their troubles, yet they hesitate to use or incorporate the community and common others into a life plan to enhance their self-development and satisfaction.

Yet, like the period of the Renaissance, ours is also a time for rediscovering the indivdual (ourselves) while revitalizing an interest in human interaction or humanness. We are striving to achieve mastery over environmental elements whether these be people, ideas, or natural and technological products.[1]

To regain meaning and control—power over the direction of their lives—many people are mustering all of their resources and are embarking on pioneer adventures to rediscover a community, common others, and meaningful communication interchanges. Some have banded together in communes, have gone back to natural ways of doing things (thereby denying technology), and have rejected professionals for the kind of help that can only come from fellow sufferers. *The mass media have served as our "navigational instruments" in these adventures.*

The therapeutic journalist, as the skilled navigator for a questing and querying special interest group, can provide beacons for the lost and guideposts for the itinerant. The therapeutic journalist can underscore involvement, association, affiliation, and purposeful activity. The therapeutic journalist can instruct in the definition and attainment of goals, can sell the importance of perseverance, can highlight the advantages of group efforts. He or she can promote social events, family activities, and community involvement. Features that inspire faith, aid educational and employment endeavors, advocate intimate relationships, can all help people overcome their sense of emptiness and dissociation.

WE NEED WORTH AND AFFILIATION

The *sixth attachment* is our connection to society through purchasing power and money. This is how we complete many transactions for environmental "goodies." This is our symbol of power, worth, capability. When we are without money and live in poverty, we are, accordingly, devalued. The person who can no longer earn money because of a disability suffers the additional burden of being detached from the community through a lack of purchasing power.

The therapeutic journalist can help the special interest group member to contact appropriate social services. The therapeutic journalist can advise how to wisely manage limited funds, shop comparatively, and invest profitably. The therapeutic journalist can provide ideas for getting a job or job promotion. Most people can use reassurance that financial and job concerns are shared ones.

Attachment five is our connection to a social role—father, mother, employee, etc. Our sense of prestige and worth is often attached to the way we perceive our roles and how our enactment of those roles is perceived by others. The most striking observation of social role influence comes when it is absent. The father who can no longer work because of a disability may suffer such a loss of self-esteem that all the other attachments are affected. The person who retires to a reclusive life is also demonstrating the importance of our attachment to roles. If one cannot at least call forth a history of successful role fulfillment, he or she will wallow, in Erikson's words (1964), in a state of despair.

Our social roles change as we progress through life. Son becomes father, student becomes teacher, employee becomes retiree. As one generation alters its roles, the next one assumes new duties and responsibilities. The therapeutic journalist can help people adjust to role changes by pointing out that our roles do and are expected to change. We all experience some anxiety and grief over status changes. We can participate in new activities, can associate with different people, can adopt new lifestyles. The therapeutic journalist as a supportive friend can help ease transitions.

Attachment four is a connection to groups of people from which we extract our role definitions. "Attachment groups can include, for example, work groups, religious groups, social groups or political groups. The dominant grouping for many persons is one based on a family, one related by kinship" (Hansell, 1974: 41). If the person can report regular activity in specific settings with groups of persons he or she feels affiliated with, then that person is connected to groups.

Attachment three is a necessary connection to other persons, for example close friends. "A person attached is recognizable when the individual is in a 'personal situation' where both parties react in a manner dependent on the past and expectable future behavior of the other" (Hansell, 1974: 39). This means the relationship has a history *and* a future.

To be successful family heads, employees, or friends, people must be community contributors and valued societal participants. When a role or the optimal performance of that role goes awry, society steps in with *gatekeepers*. These can be counselors, physicians, lawyers, and judges. When things get too unbalanced, society intervenes with trials for law-breakers and commitment procedures for the mentally ill. These rituals serve as rites of passage into the world of the shunned and shut-away. To be shunned and shut away is to be unable to participate in society and contribute to the community. Society, then, sends a mixed communication: "You will not be allowed to keep your kids unless you go to the hospital and get help"; "because you have a psychiatric history, we can't allow you to keep your kids." Society separates, classifies, stigmatizes, labels, and isolates those it rejects. Society also expects rejected people to rally and return to a respected status. People cannot do this without attachments to the community and significant others—freedoms typically not allowed the rejected person. They remain detached, imbalanced, and miserable. For this they are subjected to further treatment or isolation. A catch-22 situation, indeed.

So while the community is where we get our supplies for "selfhood and significance," a community is also the source of our imbalances and detachments. As we came to see ourselves as systems interacting with all other systems around us, we saw imbalances as environmental products more than as individual faults. Our diagnoses began to involve other systems and debilitating patterns of interaction. Thus, depression was not something the person could willfully "snap out of" but was the result of job pressures, financial problems, marital discord, or poor communication within the family. As therapists caught on to this, they began to intervene in family and marital disharmonies and would act as "consultants" in solving problems around employment, financial, social, and community matters.

It is generally recognized that the healthy person, in order to remain healthy, must be able to "move at will" within a community in order to obtain all the essential supplies for personal integrity and attachment. Wolfensberger's principle of *normalization* advises treatment specialists to help people within the community's mainstream, not away from it. Because individuals, and all other systems and their patterns of interaction, are malleable and dynamic systems, boundaries have been created to preserve continuity and consistency. Boundaries keep out undesirable inputs and control outputs. Boundaries sometimes hinder helpful blends and mixes of systems (some people are kept out of a particular group through the failure to meet eligibility or membership requirements). Gatekeepers assure boundary control through laws, mores, rules, and communication control. *To penetrate a boundary, one must always begin with and maintain a communication exchange and interchange of some sort.*

The therapeutic journalist understands that relationships change just as roles do. Some people feel locked out of families, unattached to friends, and uncertain of just who to trust. The therapeutic journalist can help people penetrate boundaries by guiding them to appropriate self-help groups, family counselors, and social groups. The therapeutic journalist can lead the audience around the community all the while pointing out where to stop, go, and exercise caution. The therapeutic journalist can be a warm and supportive friend who cares about people succeeding as friends, parents, employees, and valued community participants.

WE NEED SELF-ESTEEM

The *second essential attachment* is a clear notion of self. Having a clear identity. The information we receive and give is constantly being inputed into our identity. When the information we receive is primarily negative, or comes much too fast, it can be overwhelming and lead to identity crises.

The person excluded from society's mainstream experiences losses in dignity, independence, and community integration. According to Beatrice Wright (1960), such persons feel shame, pity, and inferiority. Because people by nature cannot accept this blow to their self-image, they will further isolate themselves and withdraw from others or will act as if all is fine, normal, as it should be in order to hide their special needs or interests from "normal" others, and mainly, the self. These *succumbing* reactions ironically only serve to make the person exaggerate the importance of his or her need or interest, thereby giving that aspect free reign over the individual's entire being. When it becomes all encompassing, acceptance by first the self and then others is hindered. The person may be, therefore, like the "man without a country": People singled out as *different* may withdraw from "normal" people so as to hide their differentness; they may not withdraw and may continually strive toward environmental accomodation and become overly dependent on the environment for affirmation of their worth; or they may withdraw only from similar others in order to avoid confronting and being associated with their special need or interest. This latter is an unfortunate reaction because through interactions with similar others we often hear about and observe coping techniques we can incorporate into our own lives. From them, "normals," and others in general, we obtain the necessary ingredients for our self-image, self-acceptance, and self-growth. Self-enhancing communication exchanges help us turn succumbing behaviors into coping ones.

The therapeutic journalist sets up self-enhancing communication exchanges. The therapeutic journalist reconnects people to significant others. He or she gets the copers to strengthen one another and to help the succumbers and those lying in between. The therapeutic journalist is really, then, an adjunct therapist who links systems in need with systems that can fill needs.

Recapping the Concerns of the Therapeutic Journalist:
(1) We need to help people have a purpose in life in a time characterized by a sense of meaninglessness.

(2) We are concerned with attaching people to the significant others in their lives and helping them to be valued community participants.

(3) We understand that when people don't fulfill socially sanctioned or designated roles, they either are treated or punished—but almost always separated. This separation or detachment, in turn, prevents people from contributing to society. Isolated people suffer identity crises and may cope or succumb. In either case the communication patterns typical for that person are altered or disrupted. The therapeutic journalist fights communication with communication.

(4) We realize that therapeutic activities are increasingly concentrating on people in interaction with others and their environment. The locus of change, therefore, is dissipated. The therapeutic journalist works for people-environment attachments and interactions.

THE NEED FOR COMMUNICATION

The *first attachment* is the dependency upon the environment for life's basics: food, air, and information. If the person is devoid of information stimuli, he or she risks personality disintegration. According to Hansell,

"Less dramatic, but equally hazardous, are the more prolonged, though less complete, interruptions of sensation which routinely accompany a confinement to bed, imprisonment, hospitalization, or certain solitary styles of life. Abundantly flowing raw sensation provides a necessary engine for experience. *Informative variety and pattern provide organization to the experiencer as well as body to the experience.* When the flow of information is severely restricted, as in confinement to bed, the attachment to information often must be considered severed, or at risk of severence" [pp. 35-36].

This is when the therapeutic journalist steps in with newsletters, radio features, and hospital close-circuit television programs.

Hansell continues, "When an individual is attached to his flow of sensation he automatically informs his social surround, using built-in affect signals, that he is seeking and reacting to that flow. The searching, scanning, and signaling qualities of the transactions with sensation illustrate the *'two-way' flow intrinsic to all the attachments"* (p. 36).

Hansell believes, then, that communication must be *reciprocal.* Just as we need certain information to survive ("this is when you should take your medication") we also need to be able to send or feed back certain kinds of information ("but I'm allergic to penicillin"). When we receive information stimuli, we have the choice to respond or not. Whatever we choose to do, we must accept the consequences that may come from our response or lack thereof.

When we have reciprocity of communication, we are in *communication interchange.* A communication interchange can be between and among people, resources, and a variety of systems. It can be accomplished by media of all types. Journalism, as the creator of chronicles of people and community interactions, completes our triad of *people in common, community* and *communication.* In fact, communication is what binds and holds together the other two components. It is the force that brings together individual systems with those of the community. It brings individuals into interaction. Good communication can give us a sense of meaning and purpose; poor communication or communication voids and deadlocks can leave us helpless, powerless, in a state of isolation and despair.

While some information is directed at the preservation of a system and can be used to protect, maintain, or enhance that system, some information—like stigma—has as its aim the limiting, separating, or demise of a system. When positive information has to compete too heavily with the negative, when messages conflict, when the individual system is left in a state of confusion and torment, we say that system is in a state of *dissonance.* It is this dissonance that may cause a person to regress, act out, or withdraw.

All communication shares the power to feed or starve—starvation coming from negative communication, mixed messages, or absence of communication (communication voids and moratoriums.) Our "boundary gatekeepers" can usually control the flow of potentially harmful information into our system or essence; our varied states of attention control the amount and kind of information we allow into ourselves. It's our boundary gatekeepers that push us to join groups or subscribe to publications that serve our needs. With a gatekeeper weakened, however, the information output can also be potentially uncontrollable. We see evidence of this in exaggerated and unwarranted behavior exhibitions.

The healthy person is free to interact with and attach to those aspects of other systems necessary for that person's definition and sense of well-being. When one interaction, or communication pathway, is disrupted, other attachments may be affected. It is like a mushrooming effect. A person labeled "sick" or "deviant," then, really is in a state of communication crisis.

People need to feel they function as an integrated unit. They need to feel this about themselves as a system and about themselves as an important part of other systems. Our sense of integrity is dependent upon our internal state of affairs but, more importantly, on the quality of the interchanges and interactions with what is outside of us. In this sense, we need to feel at home with, at one with, our environment. Communication is how we achieve this unity. Communication is, then, the act of information exchange among systems *and* the contents of those exchanges. The exchange can be easy or difficult to achieve, it can be interrupted; the contents can be positive or negative, clear or confused, understood or ignored. Qualitatively and quantitatively, communication can nourish well-being or starve it. It can do this with abstractions, plain words, symbols, or gestures. It can be direct or subliminal, intentional or unintentional. *What* systems exchange is information. *How* they exchange it is through communication interchange. When that exchange and interchange rate and quality are sufficient, the system is *attached* to those elements necessary for sustenance.

WRAPPING UP

It seems that helping, reattaching, and communicating are very complex matters. Certainly these are responsibilities that cannot be taken lightly. You, however, can perform them very effectively if you remember the following key points:

(1) The *seven essential attachments* are interdependent. A loss in one will affect others. All are necessary for the whole and healthy person.

(2) The picture that emerges of the person attached is one of a person in harmony or balance with himself, others, and a community. A state of mental and physical health is achieved or maintained when all the attachments are intact. When the balance is not severely disrupted, the healthy person can readjust to bring the system back to a state of relative steadiness. If the imbalances are severe, and efforts to readjust and adapt are ineffective, the person succumbs to suffering and despair. Says Karl Menninger in his book, *The Vital Balance* (1963), "The vital balance is thus a perpetually unstable restabilizing" (p. 114). It reconciles those forces which serve to maintain the integrity of the organism with those that strive to disrupt it. "Health and illness then become relative terms indicating success or failure in the efforts to maintain the vital balance" (Engel, 1964: 146 in a review of *The Vital Balance*). Varying diagnoses are used to designate varying degrees of imbalance. Recovery, thus, can be seen in terms of recontrol, equalizing, steadying, and balancing.

(3) Because any person seeking help comes with multiple needs and interests that originated both within and without the self, the target of therapeutic intervention should not just be the individual or a community or significant others but all of these systems in interaction and as they act upon and affect one another. The goal is to rebalance and reattach people through attention to assets and strengths of involved systems and to bring systems into mutually satisfying interaction and exchange. You can begin right now to plan ways to help your special interest group members reattach and balance by completing Exercises 1 and 2. Exercise 1 will help you uncover some of the needs of

(text continues p. 53)

EXERCISE I

SPECIAL INTEREST GROUP CHARACTERISTICS

Now is a good time for you to be thinking about the characteristics of people in your special interest group. Using the guidelines I've provided below, begin sketching your audience. Save this page because you will find it useful later.

1. The major characteristic people in my special interest group share is:
_____

2. They are usually (check all that apply):
_____ isolated
_____ institutionalized
_____ limited in interactions with others
_____ stigmatized
_____ labeled
_____ limited in community movement

3. Some of their typical reactions to the above are (check all that apply):
_____ depression
_____ withdrawal
_____ "as if" behavior
_____ acting out behavior
_____ coping
_____ succumbing
_____ deterioration
_____ other(s) _____

4. Affected attachments are (check all that apply):
_____ 1. Information. In these ways: _____
_____ 2. Self-identity. In these ways: _____
_____ 3. Connections with other people. In these ways: _____
_____ 4. Connections w/role defining groups. In these ways: _____
_____ 5. Connections w/social roles. In these ways: _____
_____ 6. Purchasing/bargaining power. In these ways: _____
_____ 7. A purpose in life and meaning for life. In these ways: ___

5. Some of their major concerns are (check all that apply):
_____ having friends
_____ having a family
_____ having a happy family life
_____ getting a job
_____ keeping a job
_____ getting around
_____ living on little money
_____ being involved in the community
_____ doing something interesting
_____ feeling better
_____ looking better
_____ being more knowledgeable
_____ having a better place to live
_____ other(s): ___

6. At least one self-help/mutual aid group exists for these people:
_____ yes _____ no
Names, addresses and phone #'s: _____
_____
_____

7. There is an Association or Agency whose function it is to help these people.
_____ yes _____ no
Names, addresses and phone #'s: _____
_____
_____

8. Other places they can turn to for help are (check all that apply):
_____ hospitals
_____ social agencies
_____ employment services
_____ educational facilities
_____ vocational centers
_____ recreation centers
_____ churches
_____ counseling centers
_____ community organizations and civic groups
_____ legal clinics
_____ other(s): ___

You can probably think of many other characteristics of your Special Interest Group. Please write them here: _____
_____
_____

EXERCISE 2

SPECIAL INTEREST GROUP COMMUNICATION NEEDS

Here are two symbols, one for your audience and one for your therapeutic
journalism medium. They are interacting and exchanging information.
Building on the examples I've written in, and what you did in Exercise 1,
begin to outline what you believe might be helpful and on-going communication interchanges

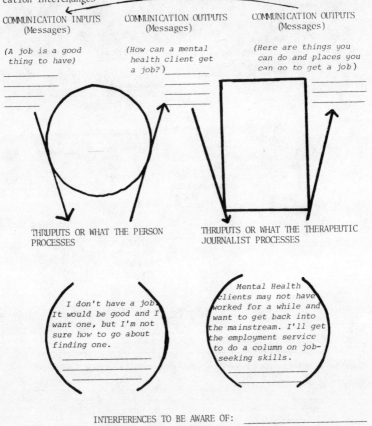

COMMUNICATION INPUTS
(Messages)

COMMUNICATION OUTPUTS
(Messages)

COMMUNICATION OUTPUTS
(Messages)

*(A job is a good
thing to have)*

*(How can a mental
health client get
a job?)*

*(Here are things you
can do and places you
can go to get a job)*

THRUPUTS OR WHAT THE PERSON
PROCESSES

THRUPUTS OR WHAT THE THERAPEUTIC
JOURNALIST PROCESSES

*I don't have a job.
It would be good and I
want one, but I'm not
sure how to go about
finding one.*

*Mental Health
clients may not have
worked for a while and
want to get back into
the mainstream. I'll get
the employment service
to do a column on job-
seeking skills.*

INTERFERENCES TO BE AWARE OF: _____

your special interest group members. Exercise 2 will help you think of ways to fill those needs through therapeutic journalism.

(4) Some University of Michigan researchers believe our time is characterized by anxiety and feelings of incompleteness and meaninglessness on the part of many people. There is a tendency to look outside of ourselves for the source of our troubles but a reluctance to take and use for our self-enhancement what's good from the outside. Perhaps people have not yet learned that what can hurt can also be used to repair. What can be a source of difficulty, if nurtured properly, can also be a source of satisfaction. The questions now are: *How* can the therapeutic journalist help people to be attached, affiliated, involved; to feel meaningful, worthwhile, and fulfilled? How can we put special interest group member into communication interchange with special interest group member; in interaction with both common others and community agencies or representatives of various types? How can we get agency to communicate with agency and then with the community?

Can we *do* something to better assure positive interactions among and across all these systems? The answer is yes, our method being through the utilization of therapeutic journalism. To this concept we are about ready to turn, but first. . . .

NOTE

1. An American Society of Newspaper Editors poll (as discussed by Thomas Griffith in the Press Section of *Time,* May 7, 1979) showed that the readers' "me" emphasis has lead to a desire for more personal and emotional kinds of journalism. They prefer the sympathetic and understanding face of the television news reporter to the bland writing and fact-stickingness of the remote and detached newspaper writers. They want, much to the disdain of the editors, a delving into people and matters of lifestyle, and these to come to life in their daily newspaper. They like hints on such things as coping techniques and eating. This "me" emphasis, confirmed by the University of Michigan studies, may be one explanation for Robinson's finding (Chapter 2) that daily newspaper readership is on the decline while TV news watching is on the rise.

REFERENCES

ENGEL, G. L. (1964) "Mental illness: vital balance or myth?" Bulletin of the Menninger Clinic 28, 3: 145-153.

ERIKSON, E. H. (1963) Childhood and Society. New York: W. W. Norton.

FRANKL, V. (1962) Man's Search for Meaning: An Introduction to Logotherapy. Boston: Beacon.

HANSELL, N. (1974) The Person-in-Distress: On the Biosocial Mechanics of Adaptation. New York: Behavioral Sciences Press.

KULKA, R. A. (1978) "Seeking formal help for personal problems: 1957 and 1976." Presented at the meeting of the American Psychological Association, Toronto, August.

MENNINGER, K., M. MAYMAN, and P. PRUYSER (1963) The Vital Balance: The Life Process in Mental Health and Illness. New York: Viking.

VEROFF, J. (1978) "General feelings of well-being over a generation: 1957-1976." Presented at the meeting of the American Psychological Association, Toronto, August.

WOLFENSBERGER, W. (1972) Normalization. Toronto, Canada: National Institute on Mental Retardation.

WRIGHT, B. A. (1960) Physical Disability—A Psychological Approach. New York: Harper & Row.

TIME OUT FOR A BREAK

SO FAR YOU'VE READ ABOUT people's needs for attachment and how important communication is to all of us. You've characterized a special interest group and have an understanding of some of its information needs, especially as they involve other systems. You know therapeutic journalism complements other journalistic endeavors and has naturally evolved from journalism's history and current helping trends.

Before delving into and developing therapeutic journalism any further, sit back and leaf through the following photo essay. When you're done, ask yourself the following questions and mentally record your answers:

(1) What affected me the most about these people? What turned me on, what turned me off?

(2) What did I learn from this photographic excursion?

(3) Is a photo essay an effective way to communicate? How could I use or improve upon this method.

Some people waiting for the bus to take them to work.

At another stop, near the hospital, alone and waiting.

"Wonder where they're going?"

"A group meeting. Mutual help. Oh, why
did I ever agree to this!?"

"I guess there's no turning back now."

"I'm either inside
wanting out, or trying
to get in somewhere.
I can never just *be there*
and have it be right."

61

"At last. I always hated buses anyway."

"Even as a child."

At the group meeting. Always a late arrival.

"We're reading the paper now."

The commuter bus gang. See who has joined the group.

"Sharing you and I are 'we.'
Our only difference may be in degree."
—Author

4

THERAPEUTIC JOURNALISM

A Need Whose Time Has Come

Presented for your reading pleasure are all the whats and whys of therapeutic journalism. Journalism as an adjunct therapist is defined.

INDIVIDUAL SYSTEMS NEED to be in interaction, to be attached to one another, to be in balance. The importance of communication in providing the means for linkage, attaching and balancing has been established long ago. We have whole books devoted to techniques for opening communication channels and keeping them positively and dynamically open. Usually we see this on the interpersonal level. Every therapeutic technique and theory that puts two or more people in interaction depends upon communication. What distinguishes one technique or theory from the others are the particular communication patterns and language used.

In all of them communication is used therapeutically. In reality, there can be no "therapy" without good communication. Yet journalism, a major means of communication message delivery, has not been considered a member of the helping team. If it has at all, it has been limited to hospital newsletters that feature the dedication ceremony for the hospital's new wing, the latest promotional highlights, and the new technological arrivals in the intensive care unit.

With journalism's willingness to expand its scope and explore new regions, with the health and mental health care systems under constant scrutiny and undergoing constant change, it seems reasonable that the two fields should establish a meaningful partnership to the advantage of both. Journalism can broaden its roles as watchdog and chronicler and become an active shaper of helping trends. Helping specialists can expand their spheres of influence by using the media. Let's examine some specific ways the partnership can operate to the advantage of both parties and certainly advantageously from the point of view of the consumer or special interest group member.

WHAT IS NEEDED

Currently, national, state and local attention is being focused on community integration for all people regardless of type or severity of deviancy or disability. Mental illness, always the condition requiring the most separation and severe treatment, is now being seen as a temporary state that doesn't necessarily call for long hospital stays or community separation. The goals of treatment now are to intervene as quickly as possible and as close to home as possible. Rather than stripping the psyche bare and slowly reconstructing the personality practically from scratch, the focus is on taking the positives and strengthening them, expanding upon the asset troops, putting healthy reserves out front. The unnecessary and harmful should, thus, fall into a state of disuse through neglect. Attention is directed at strengthening existing natural support networks, at providing linkages to systems that can be used to promote the individual's emerging well-being. Defensive withdrawal and isolation are fast becoming defunct options for the deviant.

Mandates now from many different sources are for community-based services, community-based clientele. The survival of one is dependent upon the quality of information exchange with the other. The client cannot remain in the community without adequate back-up services. The services cannot maintain a position of indispensability without records of quality service delivery and therapeutic accomplishments. The real need is for open communication pathways between helpee and helper groups at a number of different levels. We need professionals endorsing and providing referrals to consumer groups for reasons of client support. In turn, the consumers must have the freedom to call upon the professionals when the need exists and the situation warrants it. If consumers are to be left in a position of relative independence, they must be armed with sufficient information on where to go when and for what purpose. When they are there, they must be served.

Consumers have a need to know what's available to them and how to make use of the services and programs available for their use. Therapeutic journalism can help link people to what may seem to be fragmented and disjointed services and in effect may link service providers to one another. It can be invaluable in first reaching and then bringing the underserved, lonely, forgotten client into the mainstream of therapeutic and community activities.

Certainly communication is necessary for every system's maintenance and growth. Journalism is a method of choice when we can use this medium to plan, organize, carefully produce, structure, and distribute at will a variety of messages directed toward the advancement of the individual system, the community system, the network of helpers, and these three systems in interaction.

By "mass producing" messages of help and support, we can better reach into the far corners of our areas of jurisdiction and offer for the taking common currencies of experiences and matching of needs. As Gerbner (1967) believes, a publication is a creation of shared ways of viewing events and aspects of life. This can be turned around. We can use the means of a newspaper, magazine or broadcast to bring systems into an exchange of ideas, tips, techniques, experiences, and realities. When messages of this type are being used toward the goals of systemic augmentation, restoration, and rehabilitation, we call them *therapeutic.*

Therapeutic journalism is an economical means to bring individual systems (sharing characteristics) into regular contact with all the relevant subsystems of the community. Considering the scope of all that are involved, this may be a sufficient way to assure a "meeting of the minds" while allowing for personal anonymity and individual integrity.

Therapeutic journalism can be of value in unifying systems that might interact in no other way. For the bedridden person, or for the elderly person who finds it too great an effort to mingle in the community on a daily basis, therapeutic journalism can bring the most relevant aspects of the outside world in, thereby preventing or forestalling communication voids. When that medium in turn features that elderly person's poetry, mutual aid message, drawing, or letter to the editor, it is helping to achieve interaction and interchange of communication.

Besides filling or preventing communication voids, therapeutic journalism can channel communication so it doesn't grow to be overwhelming or overburdening. It can presort information stimuli, so to speak. It can take only what's potentially most helpful and offer it for incorporation and response. Therapeutic journalism, in the choice of its words and phases, can provide the emphasis on the individual that is of such current concern while encouraging that individual to attach to and balance with important elements lying outside individual boundaries. We saw in Chapter 3, in the University of Michigan studies, how people are feeling alienated from their communities and even significant others. We also saw how this gave them anxiety feelings. The person already set apart because of deviancy may not be able to adequately manage anxiety of this nature. He or she who is in some or many respects detached may not be able to withstand further severance. The deviant person, perhaps above all others, needs communication exchange and community (re)integration to repair the damage done to the self-essence. Because it is the community that created for this person conditions of stigma, hurt, and isolation, the community must redress or reverse these messages. Nothing or no one else can have the necessary impact.

Through therapeutic journalism the community can begin to send messages of acceptance and welcome. Community agencies or organizations offering help and support to people can communicate and publicize this through such features as: "Financial counseling center warns against health insurance frauds"; "extension service gives tips on living in a one-room home." By focusing on "normal" issues, matters we are all concerned with, but by adding an especially appropriate or pertinent twist, the message of aid and recognition has been sent.

In the spirit of normalization, therapeutic journalistic efforts should carry features similar to those found in other media. But these features should add something that people with special interests can identify with and use to personal advantage. For example, many media have run articles cautioning against drug interactions. But a mental health client may want to know *why* he can't drink while on tranquilizers. Similarly, we often see legal advice being given in the mass media. But the potential mental health client needs to be told he or she has a *right to treatment* as well as a *right to refuse treatment*. Another example: recipes are often found in the family pages of newspapers or women's magazines, but the diabetic is looking for great-tasting meals that he or she can safely eat. The benefits of the carefully planned hospital meals need somehow be maintained at home without the diabetic having to sacrifice those great flavors.

Messages that reinforce the positive behaviors, strengths, and assets that exist in the reader are therapeutic. They "plant the seeds" for coping, integrating, participating. They prepare people for community reentry and community interaction. They assume that people, even those with serious mental or health problems, possess self-sufficiency to some extent while, at the same time, they need some guidance on the best use of community resources. It is within the province of the therapeutic publication to outline the community's assets and to instruct the reader in their exploitation.

Resource exploitation is a standard therapeutic technique. Crisis intervention theory requires the exploration of all existing resources and their maximization regardless of trepidation, hesitation, or unwillingness on the part of the involved parties to fully activate what they have going for themselves. However inconvenient or bothersome it may be to parents or spouse—or client— the client must be relinked to natural supports. New linkages must be developed where there are deficits. This is not easy to accomplish with some people, particularly mental health clients who have been institutionalized for many years and who suddenly have had community placement thrust upon them. A whole new set of communication pathways are required; entirely different interaction patterns need to be developed.

At first the communication directed to the clients was of a staff-to-patient nature. As the patients progressed, they were allowed more freedom to interact with each other. Now the clients are being told to greatly widen their sphere of privileged others to include as many aspects of the community as can be managed.

What the client needs is not first communication at one level and then a promotion to another. Communication channels must be operating at all of these levels simultaneously. The client still needs to be educated or treated in a manner that can only be done by a staff or professional person. The client needs to share, compare, be in interchange with common and similar others. In the first case, articles focusing on professional advice, warnings, and techniques would be of benefit: "What can be expected from electro convulsive therapy"; "this is why you should take your medication." In the second case, features would be valuable that center around the philosophy of coping and participating: "Shotputting from a wheelchair"; "special tricks I learned to get the most from my artificial limb." For the last level, client communicating with community, agencies in the community should be encouraged to contribute features that are designed to educate the client on that agency's operations, potential usefulness, and steps to take in getting the services desired.

In a comprehensive system, staff communicates with clients, clients communicate with community as well as with each other. Staff also keeps a watchful eye on other staff comments and pertinent agency news. Agencies may closely follow the contributions of each other.

Don Costello (1977), writing on health communication, describes four functions of communication between professionals and health consumers: diagnosis, cooperation, counsel, and education. Actually, these very same functions must also operate between consumers and include a variety of agencies of the community such as social services, offices of vocational rehabilitation, and health and mental health departments. The recipient of a therapeutic journalistic effort will find in it *counsel* and information (education) on when to enlist the aid of agencies and how to go about getting the best services possible. Readers will be reinforced with the notion that their *cooperation* is vital in order to get anywhere with anyone. As for *diagnosis,* the reader will be helped to recognize when a recommended action is appropriate for himself or for others. For example, when consumers think their legal rights have been infringed upon in a particular situation, the feature dealing with such rights should provide enough information to outline the actions to be taken without leading the individual to a false conclusion or too hasty an action. Similarly, if a feature is focusing on the hazards of certain foods with certain medications, the person who is on that medication should be given enough information to prevent an unpleasant reaction without making the premature decision to automatically stop taking the medication.

These four communication functions need to operate on three levels just as our health care system in general must. The first level is called one of primary prevention. This is where we remove a hazard that may impinge upon that client's safety and well-being. For example, if we view a disease condition as growing out of the interaction of man and environment, as we do in the field of epidemiology, then we must intervene in that interaction to change it from one of negative to positive valence. Certain industrial wastes in the environment can present a variety of health hazards. We can educate the public on where the hazards are and what they are, and we can also publicize the need and outline the important steps for community action in attacking industrial dumping.

The second level of prevention is one of treatment. This is when we apply bandages and soothe the hurts: "You must take your medication regularly or it will do you no good." Whereas primary prevention focuses on the preservation of well-being, secondary prevention is concerned with ameliorating and curing disease.

The third prevention level is rehabilitation or restoration. This is where we feature ideas for getting back to work and sell the benefits of being in the community mainstream.

EXERCISE 3

CONNECTING SYSTEMS ON ALL PREVENTION LEVELS

Written here are the three prevention levels discussed so far in this chapter. Consider the Seven Essential Attachments and the characteristics of your special interest group you developed in Exercise I. From these, come up with some needs for each level of prevention and the agencies, people, or resources who can best fill those needs. Finally try and connect resource and need in a manner that builds on existing strengths and meets needs. Examples are provided to get you started.

PRIMARY
(Removal of Hazards)

Needs of Special Interest Group: (to avoid being alone)
_____

Relevant Systems: (family, friends, associates)
_____

Connections that will fill needs: (informal get-togethers, nights out)
_____

SECONDARY
(Treatment)

Needs of Special Interest Group: (to overcome grief over loss of spouse)

Relevant Systems: (medication clinic, chaplain, friends, family)

Connections that will fill needs: (counselor)
_____

TERTIARY
(Rehabilitation)

Needs of Special Interest Group: (to return to work)

Relevant Systems: (employers, employment service, courses on job-seeking)

Connections that will fill needs: (Office of Vocational Rehabilitation)
_____

To practice thinking about your special interest group in terms of the three prevention levels, complete Exercise 3. You will see how you are combining your knowledge of the seven essential attachments with what has just been covered in this chapter.

Great responsibility is placed on therapeutic journalistic efforts, if they are to be done correctly. Such efforts can have real impact on the active and alert interchanges among systems. The ideal situation is to have completely open communication. It is very important for a therapeutic journalist to maintain positive relations with all concerned in order to avoid a situation of disrespect and disregard.

WHY IT IS NEEDED

With the increase in size of special interest groups composed of people who are dispersed around the community and who don't have a ready means of keeping in contact with one another, appropriate professionals, and necessary services, a means is needed that can attach individuals to positive and helpful stimuli.

A means is needed that can identify the important issues, that can instruct in the use of resources, that can keep the person aware of what's around that is pertinent. The means must fit with the principles of normalization. The means should be informal, personal, and should focus on coping as opposed to succumbing. This means they should not highlight issues applicable only to weaknesses or needs, but should focus on strengths and assets as well.

We can't take people from one system and throw them to another without adequate preparation and expect a great interaction or match. We can't establish one set of communication pathways or networks and change them at will without a certain reorientation period. The communication sender has gotten used to being relied upon to send certain messages. Turn around the expectations and the result is dissonance. (When we move ex-patients out of institutions and into the more isolated rural areas, we shift the vital players or systems and confuse the communication issues.) A means is therefore needed that can provide continuous support to systems in transition. Therapeutic journalism is a piece of this support. It is not the be all and end all, but it can be important. As Allen (1978: 321) said, "treatment in the community may actually mean *less real participation* than a person would enjoy 'confined' within an out-of-the-community state hospital." Attention is called to the iatrogenic or ill effects the community can have on the individual not adequately prepared for community participation or reentry.

Ex-clients or -patients, like all of us, need to be able to make a real contribution to society. They need normal social roles. They need to maximize natural support and self-help and mutual aid. Certainly, positive linkages to and among helpful agencies are necessary, as are attachments to similar others, family members, and close friends.

We cannot depend solely on the interpersonal resources of the individual to carry the community's weight. We need the best of both worlds. We need interpersonal communication to give us day-to-day incentives, a sense of connectedness and purpose. But we also need a broader perspective and view. We need to be kept aware of what exists outside of us that can be brought inside and used to our advantage. As the University of Michigan survey cited earlier showed, people are much more self-reliant and self-oriented. Yet when they are in dissonance (receive messages of rejection and dissociation), they may chalk it up to a poor environment and withdraw from that environment. They may also act as if they were normal in order to prove that the environment has misjudged them.

To offset a lack of a sense of meaning, lack of control, people need to rediscover the community and others and incorporate strengths of these systems into their own resource and asset pool. In order to do this, people first need to be informed of what is available out there for incorporation and of techniques for achieving positive interactions with the available others. The mass media, and, hence, therapeutic journalistic efforts, are one way to get an overview of all that is around and beyond us. Indeed, it is the purpose of the mass media to provide us with navigational maps that can be used in self-discovery and the understanding of self in relation to others. Our ever-outward-expanding environment, our burgeoning information stimuli, requires some kind of check to be placed on those stimuli in order to avoid overwhelming recipients with the unnecessary and redundant. To limit the excessive flow of information that is so available, we have our special interest media directed to special interest groups. The media can broaden that special interest community and provide more sharing than otherwise possible in a "turbulent sea of verbiage." They also help to prevent communication voids by targeting information to the particular needs and interests of the special interest group.

As our world or milieu expands (as mental health clients have moved from the confinement of the institution to the geographical limitations imposed by the community's boundaries), the effective communication means have changed. No longer can mental health clients learn from one another through the ward's frequently scheduled group activities. The lack of proximity now prevents many interpersonal contacts. Hence, in order to share and communicate with one another some medium of communica- is needed: telephones, letters, or therapeutic journalistic efforts. One *why* for therapeutic journalism is, therefore, that this is the most efficient and economical means to achieve interactions and interchanges among all the systems necessary for a person's satis- fying and equal participation in unions with common others, the family, or the community in general.

HOW THE MOVEMENT TOWARD THERAPEUTIC JOURNALISM COMPLEMENTS MOVEMENTS IN OTHER HELPING PROFESSIONS

The concepts we have been discussing are not new or unknown. What is new about them is the use of newspapers, newsletters, magazines, and radio or TV broadcasts to achieve the results.

As an example of a shared point of view, recommendations will be cited from the Task Group of the National Committee for Mental Health Education. In a concept paper (Williams, 1977), it delineated the scope and purposes of mental health education in a way that indirectly, yet effectively, supports our therapeutic journalistic efforts. The recommendations follow.

There are at least four problems which the community-based mental health system has yet to solve:

(1) The vast majority of people do not want or need clinical services, yet could benefit from programs which help them lead happier, more mentally healthy lives.

(2) While many people do need clinical services, they are often unaware of community-based services or are unwilling to utilize these services.

(3) Those who are patients within the mental health system can often benefit from programs which supplement clinical services and ease the transition into therapy and back into community life.

(4) Many mental health problems are caused, at least in part, by environmental conditions which cannot be addressed through clinical approaches.

There are several appropriate areas for mental health education efforts. The major purposes and target groups include:

I. EDUCATION OF THE GENERAL PUBLIC

Education About Mental Health Problems and Resources. The intent is to create a better informed public, whose members are more aware of and more inclined to seek mental health services when needed, more accepting of others who have sought services, more cognizant of the need for such services, and more concerned about reducing the factors that contribute to mental health problems.

Education to Promote Positive Mental Health. The intent here is to develop individuals' abilities to lead their lives in a satisfying way and to have a positive effect on others. This includes such abilities as:

—growing as a person: self-awareness, self-acceptance, use of leisure time, attending to one's own needs;

—relating to others: communication, emotional exchange, self-assertion, conflict resolution;

—life management skills: planning, problem-solving, decision-making; and

—specific role skills: friend, mate, parent, employee, supervisor, group member.

II. EDUCATION OF "NONCLIENT, NONPATIENT"
    POPULATIONS AT RISK

Education to Assist People in Coping with Predictable Transitions. Such situations as marriage, parenthood, divorce, retirement, the empty nest phenomenon, discharge from military service, and moving to another community are reasonably predictable, yet they can produce sufficient stress to cause emotional problems. Education can help people cope more effectively with these predictable transitions in their lives.

Education to Assist People Living Under Stressful Conditions. Single-parent families, low-income families, persons who are living alone, widows, and the elderly live under conditions which are associated with more frequent emotional disability. Education can provide a supporting environment and the skills needed to deal more effectively with these conditions.

Education to Assist People Experiencing Symptoms of Distress. Many people experience emotional problems and are highly motivated to grapple with them but choose not to assume "client" or "patient" status. While reluctant to enter therapy, they may be quite willing to view education as a vehicle for gaining the skills needed to deal with their problems. The primary intent of programs with "nonclient, nonpatient" populations is to prevent emotional disability by building on each person's desire to maintain independence and self-sufficiency. Yet it is also likely that educational efforts will help some people to recognize the need for treatment, thus encouraging motivated self-referral and facilitating early intervention by clinical resources.

III. EDUCATION OF CLIENTS OR PATIENTS AND THEIR SIGNIFICANT OTHERS

Education to Assist the Client in Becoming a Skilled and Knowledgable Consumer of Services. This includes understanding the rights, privileges and responsibilities of a client, being aware of services which are available, and developing skills in negotiating for services.

Education to Enhance the Therapeutic Program of a Client or Patient. An educational program for clients or for their families and significant others can be an integral part of a clinical program and an important aspect of the therapeutic process. In this role, the mental health educator becomes a coworker with the therapist in helping the client.

Education to Facilitate the Transition of a Client Back into Community Life. Educational programs for clients and their significant others can ease the often painful transition back into community life. In this way, they serve as valuable adjuncts to the treatment program of a community mental health center.

IV. EDUCATION OF THOSE IN THE COMMUNITY
WHO ARE IN A KEY POSITION TO AFFECT
THE LIVES OF OTHERS

This area includes educational efforts aimed at human service agencies, school systems, law enforcement personnel, clergy, attorneys, physicians, public health nurses, beauticians, bartenders, and employers in the community. Outcomes of efforts in this area include an improved ability on the part of community caregivers and gatekeepers to be effective mental health resources in their own right and a placing of the responsibility and ownership of the mental health of the citizenry within the context of everyday life (at school, at work, in health care settings, and in relations with various helping professionals and gatekeepers). While increasing the supportive capacity of key people in the community, educational efforts should also lead to an increased ability to recognize emotional problems and refer people to appropriate resources in the community.

V. EDUCATION OF THOSE WHO ARE IN A POSITION OF
INFLUENCING AND AFFECTING PUBLIC POLICY

This area includes primarily the political arena and would focus on seeing that board members, elected officials, governmental authorities, and other key policy-makers are well informed about mental health issues, problems, and alternatives. Depending on their individual situation, educators may become involved in actively pursuing various positions with policymakers. A primary outcome of educational efforts in the public policy arena should be a greater understanding of and sensitivity to the mental health impact of all public policies by elected and nonelected policy-makers. Further, educational efforts in this area should seek to support and advance all public policies which build upon and promote mental health.

Mental health educators are not alone in recognizing the need for better communication pathways and helpful messages. There are identical movements in the fields of education, aging, and child welfare. The White House Conference on Handicapped

Individuals (which met in 1977, and which was composed of many people themselves disabled or handicapped), highlighted some important needs that could be met through therapeutic journalism. Table 4.1 puts this in graphic form. As much as could be determined from the summary of their final report, the participants seemed not to conceive of therapeutic journalism per se. The feeling is, however, that if they could have been made aware of our ideas, they would have fully endorsed them.

Thus, we have the White House Conference on Handicapped Individuals, the Task Group of the National Committee for Mental Health Education, and efforts in related areas all identifying identical needs and similar directions in meeting those needs. These recommendations can be interpreted to support the development and dissemination of therapeutic journalistic efforts.

HOW WE MEET THE NEED

People with special interests need to be informed of helpful products, services, and community agencies. We announce technological innovations and new programs. We list intake procedures and describe what particular agencies are all about. We join efforts to humanize health and mental health care services by imparting news, views, and facts to make facility contact easier and more comfortable. We provide verbal maps that enable readers to see connections among systems and their position in the overall scheme of things.

People with special interests need to be aware of their role' as consumers of service, so we feature columns on legal rights, consumer protection, consumer shortcuts. People with special interests need to feel they're a valued part of their families and the community, so we feature articles that help to sensitize systems to the needs of each other. People with special interests need to be in interaction and interchange with other systems, so our efforts provide a means where community representatives, consumers, and professionals can exchange information. People with special interests need to be given support and certain skills. We support. We teach. We tell *how* leisure time can be constructively filled.

(text continues p. 84)

TABLE 4.1
Excerpts from *SUMMARY: Final Report,*
White House Conference on Handicapped Individuals
(Some Recommendations that Received the Top Three Votes)

Health Concerns: Technology

(1) What steps should be taken to facilitate the transfer of technology so that handicapped persons receive the benefits of technology as rapidly as possible?

   (a) JOURNALS—A "Consumer Reports" type of journal for the handicapped should be established to evaluate and report on new technology; existing journals should be persuaded to report/evaluate new technology; and research results should be published in lay and professional journals.

(2) How can the benefits of new technology be published and disseminated to handicapped persons?

   (a) INFORMATION/REFERRAL SYSTEM—Some form of national information dissemination system should be developed, through such means as national/regional clearinghouses, local centers, toll-free hot-lines, consumer publications, computerized research banks, etc.

   (b) RESOURCE DIRECTORY—A resource directory "Consumer Reports" type publication should be developed to include information on technology, federal assistance, etc.

(3) How can the handicapped person be protected from charlatan technology?

   (a) CONSUMER AWARENESS—Efforts should be made to educate the handicapped to become "critical consumers," including provider training to ensure consumer awareness, publication of warning pamphlets, development of mass media programs accessible to the handicapped, etc. Consumer protection agencies should become involved, and consumer protection efforts should be encouraged through information dissemination by the mass media.

Health Concerns: Diagnosis

(1) How can we assure that effective treatment will follow diagnosis?

   (a) PUBLICIZE SERVICES—More adequate communication and publicity to enable handicapped persons to know where to go for follow-up services should be provided.

Health Concerns: Treatment

(1) How can we integrate the components of health care in order to insure that the treatment needs of clients and patients are being met?

   (a) INFORMATION/REFERRAL SYSTEM—An information/referral system should be established with a directory of public facilities and health resources for the handicapped.

Table 4.1 (Continued)

---

*Social Concerns: Psychological Adjustment of
Handicapped Individuals and Their Families*

---

(1) What psychological and social services are necessary to effect adequate transitions of handicapped individuals from an institution to a community?
    (a) TRANSITIONAL PROGRAMS—Federal, state, local, and private resources should be used to develop transitional programs including the following components: staff attitude training, sensitizing the general public, increasing normalization of institutions, shortening and/or preventing institutionalization, establishing architecturally accessible community living alternatives, and providing supportive services with counseling through peers and professionals to handicapped individuals and their families. Information, referral, and outreach services should be available throughout the states.
    (b) COMMUNITY AWARENESS/SENSITIZATION—Public and private efforts should be made to encourage media sources, authors, and publishing companies to realistically portray handicapped people in various roles and settings in order to aid public awareness and sensitization. Special efforts should be made to reach community sectors that directly impact handicapped individuals.

Special Concerns: Special Delivery Systems

---

(1) How can we get consumers involved in federal, state, and local goal-setting, implementation, and evaluation?
    (a) CONSUMER COALITION—A cooperative consumer coalition, representative of all disabilities, must be established to provide more support and power for all handicapped individuals. Funding should be provided by individual membership dues. Resources should be utilized to provide consumer information to legislative bodies.

Special Concerns: Civil Rights of the Handicapped

---

(1) What can be done to insure that handicapped people are knowledgeable about their rights?
    (a) PUBLIC AWARENESS—State human rights agencies should initiate massive public education drives concerning state handicap discrimination laws. At federal, state, and local levels, public and private agencies should inform their clients of their rights.

We identify accessible buildings. We tell *how* to deal with a rent hike.

People with special interests need to share and compare and to be helped by helping. They have as much to gain from being listened to as from listening. They need a group identity. They need to collect common experiences, needs, and interests. They need to collect their voices so that they can actively influence the programs and community aspects that impact on them. We give readers a voice that can be heard. We feature articles that will relieve, enlighten, and help to activate. We provide a means where some changes may be influenced.

The media of newsletter, newspaper, magazine, or broadcast for our messages are the ones of choice because they have already earned such wide community and individual acceptance. Some of the newer forms of media, products of the specialized press (the new journalism movement and alternative press[1]), have built a quality reputation for striving to make sense of and shoot meaning into the events and activities impacting on their readership. Publications can put all the views of many people in one resource. Generally, they can go everywhere and anywhere. Besides, it is *normal* to receive a special interest publication. We are treating readers of therapeutic publications as normal people who share something. What they are being provided is a means whereby they can exchange, compare, and share their commonness.

Marshall (1977) argues that most health professionals regard the mass media or mass communication as antithetical to beneficial health behavior. They reach the wrong people at the wrong time, they reach unnecessary people, they have no endurance or predictable saturation.

Therapeutic publications, however, are not a one-shot deal. They can be kept, stored, referred to. They can provide a regular and ongoing means of education, entertainment, self-help, and mutual aid. This is *not* to set therapeutic publications above or apart from other media—therapeutic or otherwise. On the contrary, therapeutic publications depend on other media allies in order to satisfactorily operate and impact. We must cooperate with other media. As we expect other systems to be in positive interaction internally, we can require no less of the media system we have elected to join. Actually, it's purely economic. We don't have the budgets or staff to assume the comprehensive duties of all the other media. Therefore, we must refer to them, encourage our readers to use them. How we meet the information needs of our readers is, then, by providing the best tool we can put together and by providing referrals or linkages to other media resources.

Another *how* to answer is the one questioning the tone that should be used to reach our audience. To get across the realities of coping and integrating and interacting, we must treat our reader as an intelligent, albeit frustrated, person who can take the better path once the guideposts have been erected. The hope is that through "observing" a successful model, the reader will emulate the positive behavior witnessed. We do *not* need "inspirational pleas" of the nature, "If I can do it so can you." Rather we need the tone behind the following: "This is how I did it. Maybe this can be used by you. Anyway here it is, my experience."

Becoming adept at tuning in to the proper tone, knowing what to say when, is not difficult when we take the time to get to know our readers. When we see communication as a two-way process of information exchange, we underscore the importance of mutual consultation. By going to the places our readers frequent, by getting to know their interests, concerns, and needs, we can better target communications to *their* current events. Since we will be reaching our people together and putting them in interaction, we will want to determine just what it is our people have in common. Where *they* see the community and other people fitting in with them is also important information for us to have.

Therapeutic journalistic efforts can prepare readers for community interactions, services, and treatment. Many of the sufferings that exist, and many of their exacerbated forms, are results of pressures, miscommunications, and misunderstandings coming from without. If we could intervene in communication breakdowns, somehow bridge communication gaps, and provide a means where different points of view can interact, we may help in the dismantling of some of the more insipid communication barriers that affect members of any special interest group.

Figure 4.1 graphically summarizes this chapter by delineating the many communication channels and interchange pathways

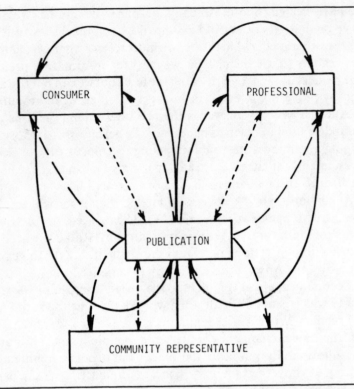

FIGURE 4.1:   Pathways of Communication Interchange in Therapeutic Publications

that must operate simultaneously in therapeutic journalistic efforts. When quality interchanges exist, the effects of debilitating interferences are correspondingly decreased. In fact, the operation of one means the defeat of the other. Through the medium of therapeutic journalism we see how consumers, professionals, and community representatives can better communicate both among themselves and with each other. Therapeutic journalism, then, serves as a catalyst in providing the opportunity for inter-action.

As a break, take some time now to review the following list on the characteristics of therapeutic journalistic efforts. When you're done, look at Exercise 4 and begin to create ways you can help people through therapuetic journalism. Now you are really becoming an involved therapeutic journalist!

Characteristics of Therapeutic Journalistic Efforts:

(1) They put people in need in interaction with people who have, community representatives, and helpers.
(2) They provide a medium for sharing and comparing.
(3) They can provide a regular contact. Thereapeutic publications can be stored and carried around.
(4) It is *normal* to receive information directed to a special interest.
(5) Media are socially sanctioned.
(6) People who are dispersed can be unified, yet can remain anonymous.
(7) The outside world is brought inside.
(8) Products and resources are identified. Utilization means are described.
(9) They can organize and presort relevant information.
(10) They can be an advocacy tool.
(11) They can support and reinforce positive coping skills.
(12) They can instruct and educate.
(13) They can reach a lot of people at once.
(14) They can ease transitions and take away "surprises."
(15) They can help people attach and balance.

It is evident that the therapeutic journalist must be responsive to the needs of the audience and be in consultation with its members to determine those needs and interests. *What* is needed are therapeutic media that aid people with diverse backgrounds to attach to and balance with outer systems through interactions with others who want to and can help, with those who share common interests, with those who just plain care. As our "communal circle" has extended outwards (as it has expanded from a patient grouping around a ward's TV to rehabilitation facilities to community integration), there is a need for a common resource that will help establish those communication pathways that allow for both broad and narrow communal cooperation, concerted means to achieve common ends, and community.

EXERCISE 4

Connecting Systems Through Therapeutic Journalism

Here are the three prevention levels again. Referring back to and building
on Exercise 3, fill in the blank lines with what you believe therapeutic
journalism can do to connect systems. I've provided one example as a beginning for you.

PRIMARY
(Removal of Hazards)

Features on community activities, ideas for easy entertaining, special benefits
from doing things with other people. Features on someone's experience in over-
coming reclusiveness, how they did it and what it was like.

_____
_____

SECONDARY
(Treatment)

_____
_____
_____
_____
_____
_____

TERTIARY
(Rehabilitation)

_____
_____
_____
_____
_____
_____

What is needed are therapeutic media with features carrying
relevant messages to those people who need help in coping with
all-too-often alien systems, a strange and unfriendly milieu. We
need features that serve to normalize expectations and reduce
dissonance. The *why* of therapeutic journalism is that the time is
right, the need and support are there, and the means are available.
The *Why* is that we can do it. Let us now explore *how*.

NOTES

1. Dennis and Rivers in their book, *Other Voices: The New Journalism in America*
(1974), give an excellent account of the history and rationale behind new journalism. New
journalists attempt to make the media a more active part of various systems through direct
involvement, interpretation, and description.

As for the alternative press offerings, so active in the 1960s, a dull thud may be all that is left of what was once a loud and clear adjuration to love and live in peace while denouncing war, competition, the establishment, and moral indiscretions. In the April 23, 1979 issue of *Time,* the following was said about our current alternatives: "Ten years after Woodstock and nearly a quarter-century after the *Village Voice* was launched as an alternative to New York City's conventional dailies, the alternative press has become so established that it is very nearly establishment itself. Gone for the most part are the radical polemics, scatological prose and serendipitously amateur design that were staples of underground journalism. In their place are entertainment listings, movie and record reviews, consumer buying guides, elegant graphics, ads, ads, ads, and more ads—for stereo equipment, records, furniture, sporting goods, liquor and other trophies of the good life" (pp. 49-50).

Of the alternative press editors present at the National Association of Alternative Newsweeklies' Annual Convention in March, "few doubted that alternatives had drifted dangerously far from their original purpose, that perhaps they were betting too heavily on special sections and entertainment guides and not enough on investigative reporting and all around hell raising. 'You have to create a product that no one else can duplicate' [warned the editor and publisher of the San Francisco *Bay Guardian*]. 'If you're sitting on your ass, thinking that you can make it on listings or a couple of entertainment articles, you're going to be out of business'" (p. 50). (Therapeutic journalists, heed this warning!!!)

Yet it may be that the pure alternatives haven't vanished but have only changed their address. As we shall see in Chapter 6, some genuine alternative publications live in the health and mental health areas.

REFERENCES

ALLEN, P. (1978) "A bill of rights for citizens using outpatient mental health services." Referenced in J. C. Turner and W. J. TenHoor, "NIMH community support program: a pilot approach to a needed social reform." Schizophrenic Bulletin 4, 3: 321.

COSTELLO, D. E. (1977) "Health communication theory and research: an overview," in B. D. Ruben, Communication Yearbook I. New Brunswick, NJ: Transaction Books.

DENNIS, E. E. and W. L. RIVERS (1974) Other Voices: The New Journalism in America. San Francisco: Canfield.

GERBNER, G. (1967) "Mass media and human communication theory," in F. Dance (ed.) Human Communication Theory: Original Essays. New York: Holt, Rinehart & Winston.

MARSHALL, C. L. (1977) Toward an Educated Health Consumer: Mass Communication and Quality in Medical Care. Washington, DC: U.S. Department of Health, Education, and Welfare (DHEW publication No. NIH 77-881). Fogarty International Center Series on the Teaching of Preventive Medicine, Volume 7.

Summary: Final Report. The White House Conference on Handicapped Individuals (1978). Washington, DC: Department of Health, Education, and Welfare, Office of Handicapped Individuals (DHEW Publication No. OHD 78-22003).

WILLIAMS, R. T. [Chairman] (1977) A Task Group of the National Committee for Mental Health Education. Mental Health Education: A Concept Paper. Washington,

DC: U.S. Department of Health, Education, and Welfare, National Institute of Mental Health, March. This is an excellent paper that attempts to unify mental health educators by providing them with some common foundations and guidelines. Well worth the stationery and postage stamp.

Part II

MAKING THE CONCEPT WORK

5

PLANNING A THERAPEUTIC
JOURNALISTIC EFFORT

All the necessary steps are covered for planning therapeutic journalistic efforts. Topics included are: setting goals, defining the audience, developing content ideas, and budgeting and funding.

PEOPLE WITH SPECIAL IN-
terests may feel anxious, helpless, lonely, and unsure of themselves. They may be unbalanced and unattached. Those who are looking for help from therapeutic journalists are looking for reassurance, helpful information, guidance to resources, and advice on how to take better care of themselves.

Therapeutic journalists, the providers of the above, are all the more likely to be successful when they present the community and its institutions as welcoming and friendly, available services as nonthreatening, and their audience as intelligent, sensitive, and capable of assimilating information that can be used to enhance the self. We should be aware, however, that to many people in need the community may not seem welcoming and friendly. Services may be quite threatening and often seem inaccessible. And your audience may be unskilled at assimilating information and using it properly. Or it may not be ready or willing to do so.

For your therapeutic journalistic efforts to be on target, successful, and useful you've got to have a pretty good idea of the community and the services it provides. Above all, you need a thorough understanding of the needs and interests of your target population.

This chapter will present the steps involved in planning a therapeutic journalistic effort. Although discussed in the context of publication production, most of the ideas you find here and in the next chapter will have relevance to any form of media you are considering using.

GELLING YOUR THOUGHTS

Before you think in terms of getting out your first issue or broadcast, it's important to decide what your first efforts will be all about. You'll want to make some preliminary decisions about the content, to be clear at whom you're aiming your efforts, and think through the matters of your budget.

One of your first steps should be to put your intentions down on paper. This can be accomplished by sketching out a four- or five-page proposal to serve as your guide and perhaps also as your presentation to others from whom you'll be seeking financial and other kinds of support. In the following pages I'll suggest what you might want to put into each of the major sections of the proposal. I'll include some examples and leave you with a number of exercise pages and forms which you can fill in with ideas for your own therapeutic medium. I'm going to begin with a statement of goals and objectives; sort of "What my therapeutic journalistic effort is all about." Logically, that's the place to begin. In practice, I've sometimes found it easier to write this section after I've thought through some of the issues which follow. If you are clear about your intentions, begin by filling out the appropriate forms in this section. If you're not, read through, jot down your ideas and notes on a scrap of paper, and come back to them later.

GOALS AND OBJECTIVES

Your goals and objectives can either be focused on the user or on you, the provider. Here are examples of both:

user-centered	provider-centered
(1) Through features directed toward the broad aims of community integration and behavior normalization, readers (sharing a particular special interest) will be reassured, informed, educated, supported, enlightened, entertained, and enhanced.	(1) To reassure, inform, educate, support, enlighten, entertain, and enhance (the target population) through features directed toward the broad aims of community integration and behavior normalization.

(2) The readers will become aware of community activities, services, and events. This awareness will increase their community participation and orientation. They will become aware of their shared needs and interests.

(2) To be population-specific and community-based and -oriented. The newspaper will concentrate on people (with a particular special interest in a limited geographical area). The newspaper will feature community activities, services, and events to make readers aware of their own community and neighborhoods.

(3) The reader will be able to identify constructive alternatives to isolation and community withdrawal through features that provide job-seeking tips, features that name the benefits of belonging to a variety of social groupings (self-help groups and community service organizations), and features that provide lexical linkages to many community resources.

(3) To provide readers with constructive alternatives to isolation and community withdrawal. Features can provide job-seeking tips, can name the benefits of belonging to a variety of social groupings (self-help groups and community service organizations), and can provide lexical linkages to many community resources.

(4) Readers will gain particular skills and the reassurance they need to live satisfying independent lives in the community. This can be accomplished through features that give health and safety tips, that educate readers on their legal rights, that impart nutritional information and money management advice, that reinforce readers with the belief they can succeed as productive community citizens.

(4) To give readers the skills and assurance they need to live independent lives in the community. Features can give health and safety tips, can educate readers on their legal rights, can impart nutritional information and money management advice, and can reinforce the belief that the readers can succeed as productive community citizens.

(5) Readers will be supported in their efforts to gain a positive sense of self and the self in interaction with others and the community. Features can link professionals, consumers, and community representatives and can put them in situations where they can exchange information and interact.

(5) To support readers in their efforts to gain a positive sense of self and the self in interaction with others and the community. Features can link professionals, consumers, and community representatives and can put them in situations of information exchange and communication interchange.

The above are some basic and general suggestions. The type of funding desired will determine the focus, organization, content, and details of your goal statements. For practice right now in constructing goal statements for your therapeutic journalistic effort, please complete Exercise 5. If you find this difficult or if you think your statements have problems, check your library for books on the subject or consult people you know who are experienced in this area. A local college or university can very likely provide you with such experienced people.

Finally, you may want to demonstrate a willingness to test your goal attainment, effectiveness, and success. You may need to evaluate your efforts to assure continued funding, to ascertain whether or not you're making an impact, and to discover what is liked most and least about your features. A survey of the type described in Chapter 8 might be sufficient.

AUDIENCE

You need to know who your audience is as specifically as possible. You made a good start in Exercises 1 and 3. Refer back to the responses you recorded there and start to think about your special interest group in demographic terms: educational level, ages, family structure, income, and also such things as how long they have been receiving services and where, whether they are institution or community based, the number receiving supplemental services of various types, common problems, and so on. These may have to be guestimates, but remember that figures do help. You can record your guestimates in Exercise 6.

From what you have just recorded, you should be getting a picture of your "average reader." This is the person to whom you will gear the thrust of your features. This is the person you will work for, inform, educate, support, enlighten, entertain, reassure, and enhance.

Professionals in the field may provide valuable insights, information, and advice about your audience. If you had difficulties completing the items in Exercise 6, you may want to consider consultation. Let's take an example where professional advice might be useful: Perhaps the readers of your therapeutic publica-

(text continues p. 99)

EXERCISE 5

GOAL STATEMENTS FOR A THERAPEUTIC JOURNALISM EFFORT

I. User-centered

The (audience) will ("have," "do") (What?)
_____(because of, through) (What you do)
_____

1.

2.

3.

4.

5.

6.

II. Provider-centered

The (newspaper) will (do what?)
_____(how?)
(for what purpose?)
_____

1.

2.

3.

4.

5.

6.

EXERCISE 6

AUDIENCE CHARACTERISTICS REVISITED

On the average, members of my special interest group:

1. Range in age from _____ to _____. The majority are about _____ years of age.

2. Have been in school _____ years. The majority have _____ _____ (High School Diplomas, Bachelor's Degrees.

3. Live ... (record percentage in each category)
    _____ alone
    _____ with their family
    _____ in a supervised place in the community
    _____ in an institution
    _____ other. What? _____

4. Derive their income from: (Record percentage in each category.)
    _____ a job
    _____ family
    _____ supplemental security income
    _____ social security disability benefits
    _____ welfare
    _____ veteran's disability checks
    _____ pensions
    _____ savings/investments
    _____ insurance
    _____ other. What? _____

5. Receive services in the form of: (Record percentage in each category.)
    _____ counseling. Describe: _____
    _____ medical assistance. Describe: _____
    _____ vocational planning and placement. Describe: _____
    _____ rehabilitation. Describe: _____
    _____ education. Describe: _____
    _____ family and social skills. Describe: _____
    _____ legal aid. Describe: _____
    _____ recreation. Describe: _____
    _____ spiritual insight. Describe: _____
    _____ other(s). Describe: _____

6. Have received these services for (how long) _____
    at (where) ...
    _____ counseling. Describe: _____
    _____ medical assistance. Describe: _____
    _____ vocational planning and placement. Describe: _____
    _____ rehabilitation. Describe: _____
    _____ education. Describe: _____
    _____ family and social skills. Describe: _____
    _____ legal aid. Describe: _____
    _____ recreation. Describe: _____
    _____ spiritual insight. Describe: _____
    _____ other(s). Describe: _____

7. Are concerned about·their:

    1. family. Why: _____
    2. friends. Why: _____
    3. finances. Why: _____
    4. home. Why: _____
    5. self image. Why: _____
    6. health. Why: _____
    7. mental health. Why: _____
    8. job. Why: _____
    9. community participation. Why: _____
   10. recreation and social activities. Why: _____
   11. other(s). Why: _____

8. Typically receive/need help in these areas from: (record percentages in each)

    1. family. Who: _____
    2. friends. Who: _____
    3. finances. Who: _____
    4. home. Who: _____
    5. self image. Who: _____
    6. health. Who: _____
    7. mental health. Who: _____
    8. job. Who: _____
    9. community participation. Who: _____
   10. recreation and social activities. Who: _____
   11. other(s). Who: _____

tion average a ninth or tenth grade educational attainment. You believe your features should be rather sophisticated. But you are advised that some of your special interest group members may be so depressed and upset that they often do not function at their optimal levels. It is suggested you gear down your publication's features somewhat to make them easier to comprehend. You are told a readability formula and index are invaluable and can be found in books at your local library (see Sources of Reference and Further Information at the end of Chapter 6). You are reminded that, in general, short, concise sentences; simple and clear wording; short paragraphs; clear thought; and the use of illustrations—all help to make your features easy and pleasant to read.

CONTENT

Now you are ready to compose brief descriptions of the kinds of features you would like to include in your publication. You may mention, too, potential contributors. For example, you have decided to run a money-managing column. You believe a local bank's public relations department will contribute as well as a local consumer group. You may want to state for each feature idea the type of contributor and point of view (professional, community representative, client) to be represented.

To discover what your readers want and need by way of a tool such as this, it may prove helpful for you to interview some of them to find out their interests and "literary needs." As a start there, and to provide you with thoughts for Exercise 7, you can kick around the following ideas for features:

Sharing and Comparing

- client-written stories, poetry, and experience-sharing features
- a help-one-another feature where a reader's question appears in one issue, another reader responds to it, and that reader's answer appears in the following month's issue

Therapeutic Resources

- a feature on therapies, i.e., transactional analysis, meditation, relaxation therapy
- a feature on medication. How to get the most out of your medication, why you should follow your medication regimen, what to watch out for in interactions
- health and safety cautions. Ways to avoid health problems and hazards. (How to read label instructions, the cons of space heaters, etc.)

Community Resources[1]

- news about local services and programs
- social calendars and dates. Activities of special note
- area happenings—i.e., places, activities, events in the community
- supplemental guides and resource directories on many areas of concern

Legal Matters

- legislation that applies to your audience
- legal and human rights column

Employment Concerns

- job placement and job searching tips; how to manage the normal pressures that exist on every job

Financial Tips

- money management advice

Nutritional Advice

- nutritional updates; eating economically but well; which vitamins do what

Home Management

- keeping up the home's appearance and comfort. Storage ideas, living in small places and spaces, getting the landlord to fix the plumbing
- simple home repairs

Personal Appearance

- personal appearance enhancers. The importance of hygiene and keeping ourselves attractive

Recreation

- physical fitness and recreation ideas for keeping active and healthy

Religion

- religious features or features inspiring faith, hopefulness, and a sense of meaning

Entertainment

- a "running" novel. Each month readers send in their ideas for the next chapter. All ideas are combined to create a novel
- leisure time fillers
- pertinent books to read
- a humor section (for comic relief)

Sports

- local games

Music

- local concerts

Art

- local shows

General

- the scoop-de-jour
- letters to the editor
- editorial section. This gives you room to connect and influence; to sort out some disjointed events or facts and combine them into a meaningful whole
- press releases. (You can actually use what you'll eventually be inundated with)

MECHANICS

You can briefly jot down the procedures behind the production of your publication so that a beginning view can be presented of the work, time, and people involved. Because this is a large and very important piece of therapeutic journalism, the whole next chapter has been devoted to production. Be aware that what you record now you might want to change after reading the next chapter.

BUDGET AND COSTS

Before embarking on a therapeutic journalistic venture (business or pleasure), you need to derive cost estimates for the type, length, and frequency of your publication. Important considerations are: costs of supplies, cost of production, cost of distribution, and costs of staff and support personnel. Exercise 8 is a budget worksheet for you. You may find it most useful if you wait to fill it in until you have finished this chapter and the next. Even then, realize that fluctuations in fortune and budget recalculations are an accustomed part of any new enterprise.

Until you have good reason to do otherwise, strive for the most comprehensive and quality publication you feel you can produce. Your publication gives an impression about you, your sponsor(s), your contributors, and your readers.

EXERCISE 7

Feature Ideas to Meet Needs of Special Interest Group

Taking what you've done in Exercise 1, 3, and 6 to characterize your audience, refer back to your notes in Exercise 2,4, and 5 and create the table of contents for your first issue. I've given one example.

MESSAGE	POINT-OF-VIEW	CONTRIBUTOR
1. (You can refuse to take medication)	(Legal/professional)	(legal aid attorney)
2.		
3.		
5.		
6.		
7.		
8.		
9.		

SOME THOUGHTS ON FUNDING

Once you have figured your financial needs, you will want to consider attracting income sources. These fall into two basic types: (1) internal and (2) external. Internal sources of income come from subscription fees and advertising accounts. External income can come from grants and contributions. External sources of aid are local foundations, public-spirited businesses and com-

EXERCISE 8

BUDGET WORKSHEET

You can fill this in based on your expectations for the first issue, first three issues, first year, etc.

<u>INCOME</u>

1. Subscriptions/sales $
   _____   ____
   _____   ____

2. Advertising $
   _____   ____
   _____   ____
   _____   ____
   _____   ____

3. Grants/contributions $
   _____   ____
   _____   ____
   _____   ____
   _____   ____

4. Fund Raising $
   _____   ____
   _____   ____
   _____   ____
   _____   ____

Total Income = $_____

<u>EXPENDITURES</u>

1. Staff $
   _____   ____
   _____   ____
   _____   ____
   _____   ____
   _____   ____

2. Supplies and Equipment $
   _____   ____
   _____   ____

3. Printing $
   _____   ____
   _____   ____
   _____   ____

4. Mailing/Distribution $
   _____   ____
   _____   ____
   _____   ____
   _____   ____

Total Expenditures = $_____

munity institutions (colleges, libraries), and local chapters of professional associations (Councils on the Aging, Mental Health Associations, National Associations of Social Workers). Contributions can be gifts or in-kind services from supportive professionals and agencies. They can include such things as the sharing of equipment, office space, phones, and secretaries. Perhaps a number of relevant agencies would be willing to form a type of cooperative where each agency chips in some of the needed revenue but no one agency has to carry the entire financial burden.

Between internal and external sources of income are activities you sponsor to generate your own income. Ideas here can come from all sorts of successful fund raising campaigns and appeals that have been held in your community. Your library can be a big help in finding out who did what for what returns.

Once you can attract some start-up funds, you can help assure your continuation by selling advertising space and charging for subscriptions. Annual fund-raising events are also possibilities. Exercise 9 lists all these potential sources of income with space for you to record pertinent notes and ideas, names and addresses.

EDITORIAL MATTERS

You will want to construct an editorial policy statement. It should be included in your proposal and should be printed in your publication both for your protection and for the benefit of your readers. It safeguards and protects the intentions and purposes of your publication. *TODAY* has the following policy: "*TODAY* should print all factual information on mental health issues regardless of whether these issues are seen as favorable or unfavorable to particular interests. The editors assume the responsibility to verify all facts before publication and to attribute quotations to their sources. Editorial commentary should be limited to signed letters or a column designated and clearly labeled for this purpose. Every effort shall be made to provide a balanced viewpoint, particularly on controversial issues."

You may also want to print alongside this your deadline and production schedule. Contributor guidelines should be accessible to readers as well.

EXERCISE 9

SOURCES OF INCOME

INTERNAL

1. Advertising

    Generated by/through: _____

    _____

    _____

    _____

    Key people/contacts/resources: _____

    _____

    _____

    _____

2. Subscriptions/sales

    Generated by/through: _____

    _____

    _____

    _____

    Key people/contacts/resources: _____

    _____

    _____

    _____

EXTERNAL

3. Grants/contributions

    Generated by/through: _____

    _____

    _____

    _____

    Key people/contacts/resources: _____

    _____

    _____

MISCELLANEOUS

4. Fund Raising

   Generated by/through: _____

   _____

   Key people/contacts/resources: _____

   _____

   _____

Next:
Using the guidelines discussed so far, you have generated preliminary plans for your therapeutic journalistic effort. You have a special interest group in mind who could benefit from features you have designed. You know your objectives and have some idea about the finances required to carry out those objectives. It's time to get it all together and make your publication *idea* a *product*.

N O T E

1. By focusing on community resource identification and utilization, there may arise unexpected interest on the part of readers in "experiencing what they've read about." So, in the summer of 1975 I got a mental health facility to donate a bus and driver to provide interested readers with a "See Buffalo Tour." This was an additional service that brought them, the community, and *TODAY* even closer together.

6

A PUBLICATION PRODUCTION COOKBOOK FOR THE THERAPEUTIC JOURNALIST

Herein revealed are the secrets of the trade.

THE FIRST STEP IN THE actual production of your publication is to get copy and illustrations. You probably now have an idea of the kinds of features you'd like to include in your first issue and what you need is "experts" in these areas to write the articles. It's up to you to decide whether you would like a professional, community representative, or consumer point of view for each particular article.

ARTICLE IDEAS ARE IN EVERYONE: THE IMPORTANT THING IS TO BE ALERT TO THEM

Getting professionals to contribute may not be very difficult. They are, most likely, 100% behind your publication and will support it and want it to grow. It is a tool they can use in communicating with their clients—another way to get their message across. To find a professional knowledgeable in the area you want to feature you could contact your readers' local association for suggestions. Local university and college departments that have concerns within the area you want to feature can also be valuable resources. Community support services and other local agencies, counseling centers, community mental health centers, hospitals, etc., more than likely have people working for them who can help you. It's a good idea to utilize as many of these latter people as possible because many of your readers will become familiar with the places, and perhaps the people who write these features, and they won't seem strange and unreal to them. Don't overlook the local VA hospital if there is one, nor other governmental centers, hospitals, and facilities. The federal, state, county, and city agencies as well as various nongovernmental agencies can each contribute something to your publication. See how you can effectively get all of these people to work together on a common project!

Community representatives, too, are usually eager to help out with a project such as this, and it's very important to have them contribute. It is more credible when the community itself shows the readers that they are accepted and that they belong in the community.

The local Better Business Bureau can be very helpful for financial management types of articles, as can local banks and other financial service agencies. Since people need money most when they are in the community (Hansell's sixth essential attachment), it's a good idea to get a community agency to give money-managing tips. Similarly with a job feature. A local employment service that readers could potentially be visiting may be willing to write a feature on job preparation and job-searching ideas. And don't forget about the rehabilitation offices in your area. Many are funded by a government system and may even have offices or facilities in local hospitals and service centers. There are also the Salvation Army and Goodwill.

You may want to include a religious column, since many of your readers often search for added reassurance and strength. Local churches or synagogues may be eager to help out. Service facility chaplains are an important resource.

Hints for easy ways to keep up the home, nutrition, and an attractive and modern appearance are columns you may want to feature. If you have a local cooperative extension that will help out, you're all set. If not, many department stores have a fashion coordinator who might contribute a feature on personal appearance. This is helpful because it will interest the reader in that store and others. And then the Better Business Bureau, in turn, can advise on careful shopping.

Many hospitals, schools, and other large institutions have nutritionists who could help out with a column on nutrition. Your local health department could be valuable here, as well as doing a variety of health and health-related topics. Your health department could, for example, list free clinics and opportunities to learn basic first aid as well as provide information on ways to get the most out of medication and ways to prevent health problems.

Recreational, educational, and entertainment opportunities are everywhere. Your city or town probably has a recreation department—your county probably has one, too, that would appreciate having its activities and events publicized. Local museums and art galleries similarly would welcome visitors. Many universities and colleges run free film festivals and sponsor various events open to the public at minimal or little cost. If you have a zoo in your area, publicize its free days if it has any. Opportunities are endless here, and any one of the places listed previously can give you leads on additional ones.

Your area Chamber of Commerce can be a valuable resource in obtaining information on area happenings and events that are inexpensive and open to the public. Area service organizations and clubs might welcome readers as members. You could feature a club and its purpose and activities, along with an invitation to apply for membership. This is a good way to get readers involved in their community. Include in your area happenings section the phone number of your local public transportation system. This will help readers find the best bus route to take to the events, places, and activities you have publicized.

Music, too, is popular with many people. Again, colleges, universities, and high schools have performances. So do churches. In the summer there may be free outdoor concerts. And humor is welcome. If you're not lucky enough to have a local comedian or comedienne, other publications may let you reprint some of their humorous material.

There are national organizations that publish pamphlets on many different topics within specific special interest areas. These can often be reprinted as they are. Many of your fellow agencies in town produce resource directories (something you may want to print for your readers in the format of an insert or special feature). Agencies listed that could be of help to your readers may spark an idea to feature them. Your local daily and weekly papers, national magazines, and TV and radio programs will all give you article ideas.

The readers themselves will give you ideas on articles they'd like to read. You may find that there's a budding author or two who would love to share poetry, prose, or an article on their personal experiences with, and within, the system. This type of article will promote sharing and comparing among your readers and will educate them, perhaps, on how to go about, or not to go about, doing certain things. It can also serve as an effective comment on the system from an insider's point of view. Reader participation and representation in the publication are musts— after all, it's their publication. The publication gives them a voice that will be heard, and in writing for others they may get in better touch with themselves.

You will certainly want to have enough material for your publication. It will help to run a brief paragraph soliciting contributions and listing the upcoming deadline. In dealing with your contributors, it will save you a lot of time and energy if you request the copy to be typed with double spacing. That way you won't have to struggle over an illegible hand-written word or phrase and you won't have to call them for decoding. The double spacing gives you room to edit.

Some, or perhaps many, contributors you'd like to have contribute monthly. To recontact them every month you can send a "contributor letter" done in memorandum format, to remind them of the upcoming deadline. It's a good idea to give them a subtle pep talk and to include copies of some of your letters of praise and publicity. This will show them how important they are.

Remember when you contact potential contributors that you are giving them an opportunity to do a valuable service to their community. Even though you may not be able to pay them, you can give them the satisfaction of helping people to help themselves. And remember also, you and your contributors and readers will have the satisfaction of working together and communicating with one another. Your publication is, indeed, an important resource and tool.

AND NOW FOR ILLUSTRATION IDEAS

Now that you have your copy, you can give your ideas for illustrations to your artist and photographer. Some of your special interest group members may be artists and may be willing to use their free time for the privilege of getting published and for the furthering of a good cause. Many community people enjoy photography as a hobby and join together in local photography clubs. Photographers in these clubs are usually quite professional and may be happy to donate photographs for the purpose of having their work exposed. Since you don't need to cut or in any way mar the photos, they may be more than willing to let you borrow them.

Photographs should be dynamic. They should be alive and tell a story all their own. They should also be contrasty—black blacks and white whites. Drawings should also be very black. If you have lots of illustrations you may want to have the artist do his or her drawings the exact size you want and can use. If they are too large, you'll have to reduce them with a proportion scale. It will save time if you can get the drawings the size you want.

BEWARE OF LIBEL

When you are arranging for and reviewing articles and illustrations it would be wise for you to brush up on libel laws. For example, accompanying articles with photographs of mental health clients identified as such should be very carefully handled because of the legal implications. (At the least you will need a photo release.) Caution applies, too, when listing clients' names in the publication in certain contexts.

Be careful of unwitting implications or associations especially when speaking of legal issues, political matters, and potentially volatile issues. What you're quoting verbatim must be verbatim. And don't take things out of context and create something new.

Legal advice is always valuable to have in questions of libel. Lawyers at community legal aid clinics, university law students, and some public service lawyers may be able to give you advice at a fee you can afford.

Before leaving the topics of contributors and contributions, take some time out to do Exercise 10. This Exercise builds on what you did in Exercise 7 and will help you to create your own "Therapeutic Journalist's Resource Directory."

HOW YOU CAN PRODUCE THE PUBLICATION

Assuming you'll want to start with an eight- or twelve-page publication (really not all that much space to fill), the photo offset process offers an inexpensive, yet quality, method of production of tabloid newspapers. Tabloids are literally "small newspapers" (each of TODAY's pages is 11 1/2 x 16 1/2). They are very easy to design and put together. They're clean and economical to produce. Most important, they are informal. They look like many papers we read every day. It is *normal* to go around town with a tabloid in hand.

You'll have the most fun and the greatest feeling of accomplishment—and also save some money—if you do the layout yourself. This is called making it camera-ready for the printer. Tips and techniques on this topic will follow shortly.

In the photo offset process, the printer makes large negatives of each of your camera-ready pages, puts four of them together, makes plates, places the plates on the offset printing press, and runs off copies of your newspaper. Because four pages go together, it's important that you think in terms of either four pages, eight pages, twelve pages, or any increments of four above twelve.

In addition to offset printing there are other printing processes you can choose. One frequently used process is *mimeographing*. It works from stencils. All of your typing and illustrating must be done directly on the stencil. An advantage of this process is that almost every agency has a mimeographing machine. A process lying between and borrowing from both mimeographing and photo offset is *multilithing*. The *letterpress* process gives a

EXERCISE 10

Resource Directory

1. Contributor contacts (writers, photographers, artists, etc.):

    a. _____

    b. _____

    c. _____

    d. _____

    e. _____

    f. _____

    g. _____

    h. _____

    i. _____

    j. _____

    k. _____

    l. _____

    m. _____

2. Contacts for financial support:

    a. _____

    b. _____

    c. _____

    d. _____

    e. _____

    f. _____

    g. _____

3. Contacts for legal advice:

    a. _____

    b. _____

    c. _____

    d. _____

EXERCISE 10 (Continued)
Resource Directory

4. Contacts for budget advice, applying for grants:

a. _____

b. _____

c. _____

d. _____

very professional look because the copy is typeset. Illustrations are generally reproduced as they are in the photo offset process.

Because anyone familiar with preparing layouts for the photo offset process can readily adapt to the other printing processes, this chapter will discuss the creation of a tabloid newspaper or offset publication. In addition, the offset process will give you high quality at relatively reasonable rates.

But the printer who gives you the best estimate on the job you want done is probably the printer you will choose. You should submit a proposal to many printers and carefully consider their bids as far as quality is concerned; what your dollar will get you, the printer's dependability, the time from when you deliver your layout to the printer to the delivery of the newspapers. Consider miscellaneous services as well: pick up and delivery, folding and mailing, and the quality of the paper stock.

You should develop a close working relationship with the printer you choose. For example, you may want to arrange to look at and inspect the negatives to make sure they are the way you want them. You should also request from him layout sheets for the size newspaper you want to produce and advice on where to get the supplies you'll need to produce the best possible layout for him, as well as yourself, to work with.

SPEAKING OF SUPPLIES

Probably the minimum by way of supplies for producing an offset newspaper is something similar to the following:

Typing paper.

Transfer lettering. This is used for headlines. It is fairly expensive and is slow to use if you're new at using it but may be

deca-dry ——— 60 PI 6760 C ——— made in U S A

AAABBCCDDEEE
AAABBCCDDEEE
FFGHHIIIJKLLMM
FFGHHIIIJKLLMM
NNNOOOPPQRRR
NNNOOOPPQRRR
SSSTTTTUUUVV
SSSTTTTUUUVV
WWWXXYYYYZZ
II123456789000
&!?$¢%// (*)..,,": ;;

HAND LETTERING 67 SANS SERIF

FIGURE 6.1

your only option unless you can find a cooperative small newspaper office or print shop with a headliner. Yet, you may be able to achieve the most variety with the transfer lettering.

Transfer lettering is relatively easy to use, and with some practice you can achieve a very high-quality look. Transfer lettering catalogues will give instructions for use.

You may want to invest in a number of sizes, and styles, to add variety to the appearance of your pages. Consider staying within one "family" of faces. For example: Futura Bold Italic, Futura Medium, Futura Bold Condensed. A variation in sizes also allows you to put smaller headlines with shorter articles.

You don't really need to invest in a burnishing tool, which, in general, is used to apply pressure that makes the letters stick to

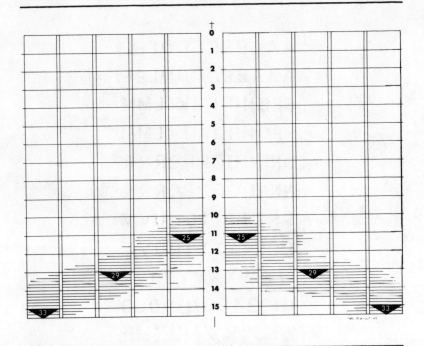

FIGURE 6.2

the paper. Here it's used to make the letters transfer. A ball-point pen that has run out of ink will work nicely in forcing the letters onto the paper.

You can also use transfer lettering to produce your subheads and kickers (defined soon) and whatever else you want to stand out. Once a headline or whatever is made, you can use it again in part or whole.

Layout sheets are available from your printer.

A *wax coater* is used for coating the backs of your headlines, etc. and typewritten pages with a wax that will fix them to the layout sheets. The wax coater covers your material with a coating composed of tiny peaks so that it will adhere strongly but not permanently. When the waxed material is not heavily burnished down, it's easy to lift it off the layout sheet and place elsewhere. The smaller, hand-held type of wax coater is the least expensive.

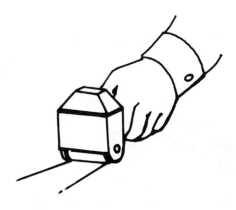

FIGURE 6.3

A carbon ribbon typewriter is hopefully already available in your office or accessible somewhere nearby. The carbon ribbon is the one that you "use once and throw out" and always seems to be running out. It has real advantages over cloth ribbons because it types crisp, sharp letters. A cloth ribbon will generally do, but perhaps you should ask your printer about it while showing him samples of how it types.

Typewritten copy can save you time and money. It lends an air of informality but, if done on an IBM machine, can be laid out to look very professional.

Blue pencils should be light but not invisible. But it is important that they be invisible to the camera. The camera (remember the plates are made from negatives) doesn't detect a light blue color, so you can use one safely to make notes on the final copy.

This is a tool you will use to make your margins on the typing paper, the layout sheets, and for making proof marks on your typewriter copy. They can be used for anything you want to notate that you don't want to show up in the newspaper.

Knives with paper-cutting blades such as *X-acto knives* make quick, straight, and clean cuts.

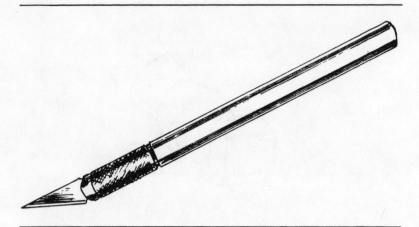

FIGURE 6.4

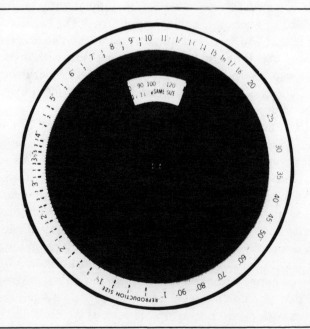

FIGURE 6.5

FIGURE 6.6

A Proportion scale is used to scale down or enlarge your photographs in proportion.

Red acetate or black construction paper is used to denote the exact size of the photographs you want in your paper and exactly where you want them. Your proportion scale determines the size of this.

A T-square is an invaluable aid in getting straight lines. A metal one is best because you can cut against it and not damage it.

Ruler.

White correction fluid is used for last-minute touch-ups on stray dark marks you want to cover up.

Border tape is used for making borders, boxing in articles, underlining for emphasis, etc.

FIGURE 6.7

Many of these supplies are available in art stores and from graphic arts suppliers. If you're not sure how to use any of the above supplies, your printer or supplier can show you how and provide additional advice and useful hints. Exercise 11 gives you a production checklist.

GETTING READY FOR THE LAYOUT

The first essentials are typewritten copy and headlines, kickers, subheads, and illustrations. Now prepare your typing paper for typing. Once you know your column width, it is recommended you mark these off on the typing paper with your blue pencil. This serves as a guide for the typist so that the copy remains within the columns and letters don't overextend. If they extend too far beyond the margin, they may run into the next column even though you leave lots of space in between the columns. It's best to stick to one typewriter face to avoid a confusing-looking layout. When you get your copy back from the typist, be sure to check for typographical errors. Names, dates, and figures should get special attention.

Your columns can be justified or unjustified. Unjustified (ragged or ragged right) columns lend an air of casualness and informality—desirable for this type of publication—as well as being less time-consuming to produce.

(text continues p. 125)

EXERCISE II

PRODUCTION CHECKLIST

	PRINTER A	PRINTER B	PRINTER C
1.	Process _____	Process _____	Process _____
2.	Cost for 1,000 copies _____	Cost for 1,000 copies _____	Cost for 1,000 copies _____
3.	Cost for additional 1,000 copies _____	Cost for additional 1,000 copies _____	Cost for additional 1,000 copies _____
4.	Quality rating from samples seen _____	Quality rating from samples seen _____	Quality rating from samples seen _____
5.	Hours from layout delivery to run completion _____	Hours from layout delivery to run completion _____	Hours from layout delivery to run completion _____
6.	Delivery charges _____	Delivery charges _____	Delivery charges _____
7.	Other charges _____	Other charges _____	Other charges _____

Add 2,3,6 and 7. This is Total(A)

Total(A) _____   Total(A) _____   Total(A) _____

Find Out What Supplies You'll Need, Where You Can Get Them and For How Much?

Equip/Supply	Supplier 1 2	Cost 1 2	Equip/Supply	Supplier 1 2	Cost 1 2	Equip/Supply	Supplier 1 2	Cost 1 2
_____			_____			_____		
_____			_____			_____		
_____			_____			_____		
_____			_____			_____		
_____			_____			_____		
_____			_____			_____		

(B) Total of Best Prices* $ ——   (B) Total of Best Prices* $ _____   (B) Total of Best Prices* $ ____

+ Total (A) _____   + Total (B) _____   + Total (B) _____
= Total (C) _____   = Total (C) _____   = Total (C) _____

*Be sure to take into account warranties and guarantees, service charges, supplier dependability, etc.

Add the total of best prices to Total (A). Compare result to items 1, 4 and 5. Go back to Exercise 8 and see how you're doing. Say a prayer, pick a printer, and buy supplies!

JUSTIFIED COLUMN

 What makes one human being
different from another? Is it his
physical, cultural or mental state?
Why is it that some will reach out
and help you -- while others only sit
back and watch?

 As I go about my everyday life
I ponder these questions in my mind.
Not because I am so much in need of
an answer; but because I am so glad
that I came in contact with some of
those persons who did not allow my
physical, mental or cultural make-up
be the determining factor as to
whether or not they would reach out
to me.

UNJUSTIFIED COLUMN

 What makes one human being
different from another? Is it his
physical, cultural or mental state?
Why is it that some will reach out
and help you -- while others only sit
back and watch?

 As I go about my everyday life
I ponder these questions in my mind.
Not because I am so much in need of
an answer; but because I am so glad
that I came in contact with some of
those persons who did not allow my
physical, mental or cultural make-up
be the determining factor as to
whether or not they would reach out
to me.

FIGURE 6.8

Dog Days   *Today's Pharmacy*

Baseball is Back in Buffalo!

The `Rock Pile´ is Transformed   *War Memorial Stadium*

FIGURE 6.9

As mentioned before, carbon ribbons will give the best reproduction. If you don't use a carbon ribbon, show your printer samples of the quality your ribbon produces and ask for his advice and suggestions.

While the typist is typing, you are ready to do your headlines with the transfer lettering. You'll need your T-square, ruler, and blue pencil. Make straight lines with the blue pencil and leave enough space between lines for your letters to fit without being crowded. The blue line now serves as a guide in keeping the letters straight. Spacing between words should be no more than the letter e. Spacing between letters should be minimal.

Often with transfer lettering the letters "transfer" when and where you don't want them. A rubber eraser found on the end of almost every pencil will easily erase them. This can also be done when a letter is out of line. It prevents having to do a whole word over or cutting it.

An additional method that will remove unwanted characters or lines is to cover them with a clear part of the transfer lettering sheet and trace over it a few times. It will readhere to the sheet. Remember this—it may save work. Another frequent unpleasant occurrence is white space, holes, or cuts in the letters. You can fill them in with a black pencil or pen.

Now you can get together your blank layout sheets and use your ruler, T-square, and blue pencil to mark off the columns you want—if they are not already there or of the size you want. It is wise to continue your blue line for the full length of the layout sheet because in laying the copy down, you may cover some of the blue line you need to line up your border tape with the columns.

For a tabloid newspaper, a three-inch column page works out nicely. TODAY uses three unjustified columns of three inches. This leaves half an inch between columns, which is sufficient.

HOW TO DO THE LAYOUT

You should strive for an informal, uncluttered, attractive layout that has no large masses of type. Type can be broken up with illustrations and/or white space. Paragraphs should be short. You should produce as neat and clean a layout as you can because with this printing method "what you see is what you get."

Now for the actual mechanics of producing a layout. You are ready to begin filling your blank layout sheets. You will probably be given layout sheets by your printer if you request them, with each sheet including two full pages. These will have to be numbered in a special sequence so that when they are run off the press, they will fall in order in the final copy. For a twelve-page tabloid, the pages should be numbered as indicated in Figure 6.10.

On your layout sheets make your column lines, if not already there. Now your job is simply (!?!) to get everything you want in the paper to fit—in an attractive and easy-to-read way. You've seen newspapers, and the basics are pretty much the same: Taking first things first, your banner (title, date of publication, volume number, name and address of your sponsor(s), and other identifying information on the top of the first page) should be uncluttered and attention-getting. This is where you may want a unique type face or design that will set off the title of your publication.

The entire front page takes priority. The contents you place there must be of very high quality. The front page layout especially should be eye-catching and visually very appealing. People should say, "This looks interesting. I'm going to pick it up."

FIGURE 6.10

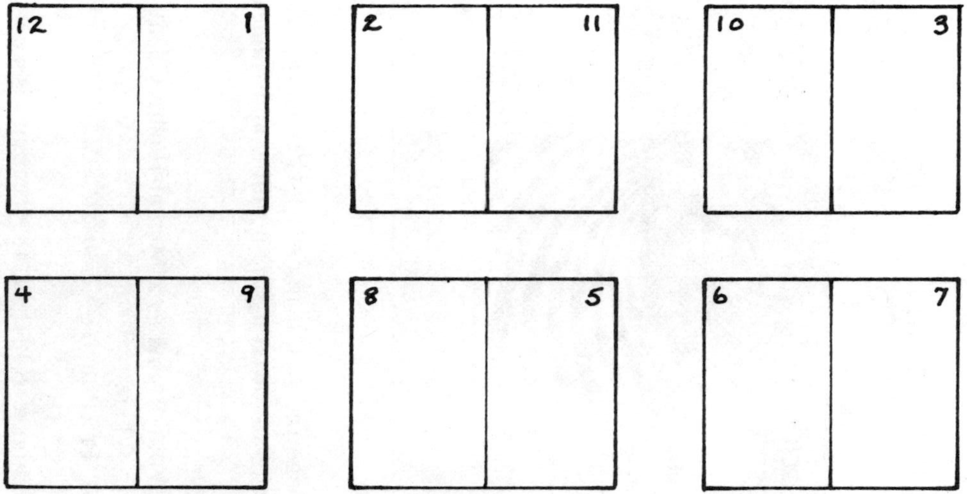

Your Mental Health
In Your Community

August, 1975

Published by the Mental Health Association of Erie County, Inc.
1200 Elmwood Avenue, Buffalo, New York 14222
Supported by:

Vol. 2 No. 6

Erie County Department   Buffalo Psychiatric   United Way
of Mental Health   Center   of Erie County

"Being back home wasn't easy"

Janette tells why

Already I have spoken of my hospitalization in Virginia and my move to Buffalo as a temporary stay to get my daughter. As I mentioned in the previous article, my husband changed his plans and came here from California. Before he arrived I went through a crisis.

Since the plans we had did not include staying in Buffalo, I saw no reason to begin therapy in Buffalo. The doctor I had seen in Norfolk had recommended that I continue therapy. The short time I

ignored our hosts and were inconsiderate. Tension increased

Jean's Journal

The purpose of this journal is to pinpoint the reasons you are here. It is important that you go back to the days prior to your admission and, with reference to time, place and persons involved, sort out the behavior that led to your admissions in this hospital. Once this task has been completed you should work on explaining your behavior during this hospital stay. You must work at gaining insights into yourself, in contacting and holding onto the real events, the real places and the real persons involved. To help refresh your memory you will be allowed to read your chart, preferably in the company of your therapist. You might misunderstand some statements and it is important that they be clarified before dark imagination wring them into something unbearable or distorted.

GOOD LUCK JEAN

FIGURE 6.11

For that page and all the others, a kicker may appear at the top of your articles followed by the headline and subhead. For example:

kicker: Your Rights as a Mental Health Client
headline: Where to Live
subhead: Freedom To Choose???

Notice in Figure 6.13 how the headline is kept within the boundaries of the article. A head should never extend beyond the width of an article's copy.

The placement of your features and illustrations is important. Some say the eye moves from the upper left corner of a page in a diagonal direction to the lower right. Given this, it's best to use the lower end of the page for incidentals.

Your Mental Health
In Your Community

FREE

February, 1977

Published by the Mental Health Association of Erie County, Inc.
366 Forest Avenue, Buffalo, New York 14213
Supported by:

Vol. 3 No. 12

Erie County Department of Mental Health   Buffalo Psychiatric Center   United Way of Erie County

Mental health clients in the community:

Three points-of-view

Professional

We've all heard many comments about clients being "better off" in the community. For most persons who need treatment for emotional problems this is true. If we can compare hospitalization for a mental disorder to a physical illness, a short stay in a hospital is sufficient for recovery. The person then is able to assume his normal patterns, working, studying, living with his family, taking part in various social circles, etc.

However, the idea of a short stay in a mental health facility is still not universally accepted. In our society there prevails the idea that persons with mental disorders need to be put away and kept under surveillance until all parties involved are assured that the patient is "cured."

The long hospital stay may in itself create a dependency on the institution where everything is planned for the person and all needs are provided. Meals are taken at a prescribed time, clothing is provided, shelter is provided. Leisure time activity is scheduled. Little change can be expected.

The Mental Hygiene system has made significant strides in changing some of these patterns. The creation of neighborhood centers for service to clients close to their own homes is in effect and more successful than is realized.

The out patient clinics, community based service teams, and day care continued on page 8

Client

A Pilgrim's Progress of Mental Health

Our pilgrim is a client of a mental health facility and what we are about to do is look on as he progresses within the Mental Health system, so that we can know just exactly what his journey is about. The client takes his first steps; he is: diagnosed, prognosed, medicated, bathed, showered, sprayed and scented.

Validated as indeed a client, he progresses to the next level where he is nursed and dressed, cursed and blest, rested, tested, and so on.... and along with other things becomes: exposed to visits from relatives not really welcome, driven to co-habitate with some very unusual people; some more unusual than himself, evaluated by vocational experts, on whose tests he scored especially well in hospital continued on page 4

Community resident

One year ago I would have thought that the idea of deinstitutionalization was as American as motherhood and apple pie. I still favor the notion of integrating mental health patients into the community, but my experiences of the last year have made me more cautious and more aware of possible defects in the process.

My primary concern is with the way these community facilities are established. My neighborhood is now called "oversaturated" because agencies set up homes without consulting one another and without consulting community residents. I found out about one half-way house quite by accident. I was ready to call the police about a man I'd seen aimlessly wandering around the neighborhood for two days when I was walking my child to and from school. Fortunately, a shopkeeper told me to check with the "house" down the street. In other instances when there were problems at a facility, neighbors did not know which agency to call and so could only call the police. Less than two months after my introduction to deinstitutionalization a different agency bought property less than a block from another half-way house, without knowledge of its existence and without notifying the community or its elected officials.

I understand that the goal of deinstitutionalization is to integrate clients into the community. If this is true, then I believe the community should be informed and educated to continued on page 3

FIGURE 6.12

2 Your rights as a Mental Health Client

Where to live

Freedom to choose???

by
Roger Stone
Consumer Advocate
Crisis Services

Q.   Recently I have heard very much about the power of local communities to exclude mentally disabled persons wishing to live in group homes through the use of discriminatory zoning ordinances. What can be done about this type of discrimination, which in my mind is no better than refusing to allow persons to live in a community because of their color?

A.   This is a very complex question and it is impossible to give you a complete answer. To begin with, not all types of discrimination based

local government can fully justify the use of discriminatory zoning patterns to enhance or protect the health, safety and/or welfare of its citizens. In addition, the zoning ordinance must be reasonably related to a valid public purpose. Zoning has long been viewed to be within the power of local governments in order to regulate housing patterns.

In 1974, the United States Supreme Court held that zoning which discriminated against unrelated college students residing in a "single-family residence" was legally permissible. The decision in determining whether a group home fits the definition of "single family residence", and whether the unrelated persons residing in such a home can be deemed to constitute a "family" can only be made upon a case-by-case basis. In

A California court has recently ruled that the city of Los Angeles may not use its zoning power to exclude State-authorized family or group homes serving six or fewer mentally handicapped persons. In addition, a New York appeals court has very recently ruled that a group home for mentally retarded children constitutes a "family" for zoning purposes, and thus cannot be excluded from a "single family" residential area. In this case, the court took note of "the recent trend... toward the establishment of community residence programs for the mentally disabled, including "mentally retarded children", as an alternative to institutionalization."

Even where zoning ordinances attempt to regulate the establishment of group homes for the mentally disabled, based upon valid zoning considerations, there can often be found legal shortcomings with the zoning plan. Therefore, each case must necessarily be analyzed upon its own facts and circumstances, and no general answers can be provided which will define when a local zoning board has overstepped its

FIGURE 6.13

Photographs should move onto the page, not away from it (the reader's eyes will follow the direction of the photo). Be alert, too, to how the fold will affect the impact of the photo. For variety, you can try an occasional reverse. What was a black background with a white and light grey figure will now have a white background with a black and dark grey figure.

To keep the top of an article from looking too cluttered, you may want to run the by-line at the end. Articles can be continued on the following pages, but too many "jumps" lose the reader.

It is useful to run articles for two or more columns, but it is standard procedure never to run an article as illustrated in Figure 6.14. Here the article begins low in this page's left-side column and continues in the next column higher than the headline. It should go something like the right-hand example.

Coupons should always appear in an outside edge or corner. They are too difficult to cut out if they are in the middle of a page. Your border tape will effectively separate articles, as will good

(text continues p. 132)

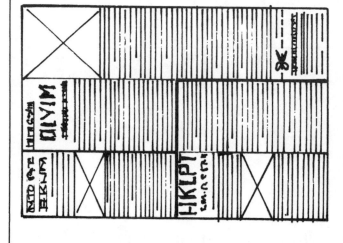

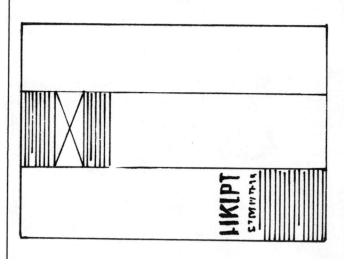

FIGURE 6.14

131

EXERCISE 12

LAYOUT DESIGNS

From the features you listed in Exercise 7, plan the layout for a 4-page publication. I've gotten you started with your pages. You put in your columns and copy and illustrations.

4	I

2	3

use of white space, decorative designs, illustrations, boxes, and screens (your printer will tell you how to designate areas for this grey shading). These are only a few hints. As you go along you will discover some of your own. (You can practice right now in Exercise 12.) If you have questions your printer is always a great resource.

Now you are ready to burnish down your layout (technically a "camera-ready mechanical" at this point) and give it to your printer. The rest is up to him. When you get your final copies of the paper, you will have to distribute them.

THE FINAL STEP: DISTRIBUTION

You'll want to get copies of the paper in as many places as possible for maximum exposure, utilization, and impact. A list of relevant agencies is a good start. Each can be contacted to see if they would be interested in receiving copies in bulk to distribute individually to their clients. If so, ask how many they would like to receive each month. Libraries are a must—both public and privately held collections.

If you're lucky, you'll have some volunteer help to draw upon for distribution of the bundles of papers to the various interested agencies. If not, and you have a car, you have a solution. If you're even luckier, the agencies will come to you to pick up their issues.

If you want to build a mailing list, publicize that fact in your newspaper. When you get a large mailing list, you can check with your post office for special rates you may qualify for.

If you start out hand addressing your papers and the size of the mailing list makes this no longer feasible, see if you can interest an agency in letting you use its addressing machine. This will save you time and money and gives that agency a chance to actively support your efforts. After all, cooperation is what this is all about.

Above All:
There are many people to whom you can turn if, after reading this chapter, you have many unanswered questions and concerns about production or anything else to do with your publication: your printer, experienced newsletter or newspaper people, professionals in your field, and textbooks on various aspects of editing, writing, graphic arts, photography, printing, etc. Sources of assistance are all around—the important thing is to be open to their suggestions, and most importantly, to the wants and needs of the readers you are serving.

SOURCES OF REFERENCE AND FURTHER INFORMATION

The Associated Press Stylebook and Libel Manual is available from:

> The Associated Press
> 50 Rockefeller Plaza
> New York, New York 10020

U.S. Government Printing Office Style Manual is available from:

> Superintendent of Documents
> U.S. Government Printing Office
> Washington, DC 20402

Both are filled with tips on "how to tell it and write it" so it's socially and legally acceptable.

A Word Division Guide is available from the U.S. Government Printing Office.

Pocket Pal: A Graphic Arts Production Handbook is available from:

> Pocket Pal Book
> P.O. Box 100
> Church Street Station
> New York, New York 10046

This is an excellent and comprehensive beginner's guide.

Burke, Clifford, *Printing It: A Guide to Graphic Techniques for the Impecunious* (Berkeley: Wingbow Press, 1972). Available from:

> Book People
> 2940 Seventh Street
> Berkeley, CA 94710

All the whys and hows of offset printing.

Editors of the Harvard Post, *How To Produce a Small Newspaper: A Guide for Independent Journalists* (Boston: Harvard Common Press, 1978). Available from:

> The Harvard Common Press
> The Common
> Harvard, MA 01451

This book is remarkably similar in style to this chapter (my only defense is that I preceded them by three years). They go into much more depth than I have done here and include discussions of copyrighting, advertising, and present good ideas on keeping the books and records straight. They also cover the area of subscriptions.

Readability formulas help you to determine the level of education your written materials are addressing. A good one because it's easy to use is:

Fry, Edward, "A readability formula that saves time," *Journal of Reading,* Vol. 11 (April 1968), pp. 513-516.

Fry's formula has been improved by:

Kretschmer, Joseph, "Updating the Fry readability formula," *Reading Teacher,* Vol. 29 (March 1976), pp. 555-558.

Two of the Sage Human Services Guides that might be particularly helpful to you in attracting income and feature ideas are:

Volume 1, *Grantsmanship* by Armand Lauffer

Volume 6, *RESOURCES for Child Placement and other Human Services* by Armand Lauffer.

Both are user's guides to generating income and attracting a variety of supporters and resources. Both can be ordered directly from:

> Sage Publications, Inc.
> 275 South Beverly Drive
> Beverly Hills, CA 90212

For help in gaining technical skills, check out adult education or continuing education courses at local educational facilities.

Your library is always a good resource.

And don't forget such common tools as a dictionary and thesaurus!

7
THERAPEUTIC JOURNALISTIC ALTERNATIVES

Examples of therapeutic journalistic efforts and ideas are given to stimulate your creative thinking.

IN CHAPTER ONE THE SUC-
cess of one therapeutic publication was mentioned—mine. It can not be stressed too much, however, that critiques can be as much a part of a publication's life as its compliments. While *TODAY* has received support and commendation, it has also been questioned and criticized.

One of the most outstanding criticisms that comes to mind is one made by a former mental health client who went on to achieve a degree of national recognition for a book she wrote on patient-controlled alternatives to mental health services. Some of her comments were: "I am not particularly interested in material prepared for clients by others, but in activities involving ex-patients only. . . . I find it most distressing that your publication promotes the same old discredited idea that others must speak for patients. Patients can and are speaking for ourselves."

She, of course, missed the therapeutic journalistic point but did underscore in my mind the importance of having our readers decide for us what *their* resource will include, highlight, and promote.

So, to provide you with choices and options in considering ideas for and approaches to the therapeutic publication you decide to coordinate, I herewith present examples of a number of diverse special-interest publications. You can select what you think are the best features of each and write to the editors of the publications you are most interested in.

AUTHOR'S NOTE: *The author expresses grateful appreciation to the editors who so cheerfully provided information on their publications.*

READ ALL ABOUT IT: JOURNALISM HELPS THROUGH MANY PUBLICATIONS

People with special interests are becoming more visible and are asserting their rights in a variety of areas. To supplement the formal help system, many are banding together in mutual support, self-help, or political action groups. Publications have been developed by these groups as a medium for information-sharing, information gap-filling, group cohesiveness, and consumer education. Some varied examples of publications follow with brief descriptions to highlight their major thrusts and points of view.

The publications listed are those for which recent copies could be obtained. Publications tend to come and go depending on interest and finances. Sadly, some very good special-interest publications have died in the past few years. A sample of some current publications will be noted in this chapter and the Appendix, which lists the publications' place of contact and "vital statistics."

Before describing these publications, it should be mentioned that only a smattering are included. Besides the obvious limitation of space, there is the fact that there may be many more examples of this type of creative journalism that have not come to the attention of this author. Hence, this chapter should not be taken as any particular endorsement of publications listed or any criticism of those omitted. Those included do, however, illustrate typical characteristics of special-interest publications.

THE EXAMPLES

The Independent published by the Center for Independent Living in Berkeley, California, is a good example of a special-interest publication with a self-help orientation. It's audience is composed of people with disabilities, and it features legal news and views, medical and equipment innovations, and "testimonials" from those who have "made it" in some way and who are willing to share how they did it with others. *The Independent* has run a variety of consumer education features centered on such

FIGURE 7.1

goals as making it financially and getting around more easily. Through sharing and helping one another, readers can develop a strong sense of group solidarity.

The Independent Observer not only shares a similar name with *The Independent* but has a like orientation. It is a newsletter for handicapped students of the State University of New York at Buffalo. The goal is to share and compare so as to make student life easier for all disabled students. Important issues are accessibility of university facilities and accomodation of the institution to the needs of this student population. Tapes of the newsletters are made available to students who are visually impaired.

Madness Network News, a tabloid, is the "quarterly journal of the psychiatric inmates anti-psychiatry movement." The one issue I saw featured somebody's discussion of "My Career as a Profes-

FIGURE 7.2

sional Mental Patient," a plea for the mentally and physically
disabled to aid and advocate for one another, a personal view of
the "Mental Patient Movement in Holland," and a hefty miscellaneous assortment of legal matters of interest. I like the word
"Network" in the title because I think this paper helps to link a lot
of people who share unpleasant experiences with hospitals and
psychiatric services.

One regional spin-off to *Madness Network News* is *Constructive Action for Good Health Magazine*. Coming out of Syracuse,
New York, it advocates "personal SELFHELP and SELF-
HEALTH methods to excellent mental, emotional and physical
health." It also features articles and philosophies of the nature of
Madness Network News. Right now it is a mimeographed publication.

AA Grapevine is the "International Monthly Journal of Alcoholics Anonymous." It too is a linking resource for fellows, but has a more traditional and positive feel about it. Testimonials, sharing, and comparing are the major themes. There is also a humor section and some inspirational and educational features. I know people who swear by this publication.

Other organizations too rely on a publication to keep their members hopeful and well informed. The *NSAC Newsletter* is produced by the National Society for Autistic Children and is "dedicated to the education, welfare and cure of all children with severe disorders of communication and behavior."

Paraplegia Life is from the National Spinal Cord Injury Foundation and features program highlights, convention reports, and other organizational newsletter topics. Yet it adds a new dimension to the "annual report" type of writing that typifies many monthly publications by keeping readers informed of new research findings and programs, legal issues, and product innovations. It also recognizes famous paraplegics, provides tips on personal care, and discusses attitudinal and miscellaneous concerns.

As spin-offs to *Paraplegia Life,* many local chapters of the National Paraplegia Foundation have their own publications. When writing to *Paraplegia Life,* you may wish to ask for the address of a local chapter.

The GREEN SourceBook is an annual published in Winter Park, Florida by SourceBook Publications, Inc. Basically, a "Directory of Products & Services for the Disabled," special features are included that focus on working out successful environmental accommodations. Some past articles have discussed topics such as "Keeping Warm in Winter When One has Circulation Difficulties," "California's Blue Curb Law," and "Shotputting from a Wheelchair." Special "Green Papers" will be issued from time to time to subscribers covering such topics as interpretations of new laws affecting the disabled and new breakthroughs in other phases of rehabilitation.

The above are all publications designed for particular groups by their fellow group members who, at least partially, control editorial decisions. Health communications professionals too are now either directly addressing people with special interests or are keeping a more general audience on the right health tract. Publications have progressed from listing the menu for the week and the dedication ceremony for the hospital's new wing to highlighting practical ways for consumers to become more independent and satisfied in their community.

MMC Focus on Health, published by the Metropolitan Medical Center in Minneapolis, Minnesota, runs bi-monthly features such as, "Stocking the Home Pharmacy," "There's no Mystery in Reading an Rx." The editor of *Focus on Health,* Candy Johnson, says, "I try to include stories that deal with health concerns the average reader might have. Many of the articles use the ' how to ' approach in improving one's lifestyle such as how to interpret dreams, how to use leisure time more creatively, or how to develop an exercise program."

As an example of the new kind of "hospital newsletter" being produced nowadays, attention is called to *Outreach,* published by the Ohio State University Hospitals. *Outreach* builds much human interest into its pages. Programs, achievements, and people are described as they affect people. For example, in an article titled "New Treatment Tested for Sickle Cell Anemia," the emphasis was not so much on the treatment per se as the people who did and who will benefit from the treatment.

If we take a broader look at special-interest groups, two publications stand out. One, called simply *NEWS,* is produced by the New York State Office for the Aging to keep senior citizens informed of legislation and legal rights as well as programs and events of interest.

The *Health Law Newsletter* is published by the National Health Law Program and is "distributed free to Legal Services clients and attorneys and to health providers and consumers who wish to learn about health-related problems of the poor."

Focusing specifically on the interests of self-helpees and self-helpers, the *Self-Help Reporter* features articles relevant to members of self-help mutual aid groups as well as professionals involved with such groups. This newsletter contains short news items of interest, essays, and lists of materials available.

Finally, there are two publications noteworthy for their discussions of therapeutic alternatives: *Institutions, Etc.* is a monthly compendium of investigative articles on institutions (mental hospitals, prisons, etc.) and their alternatives. *The Choice* is the official publication of the Committee for Freedom of Choice in Cancer Therapy, Inc. and, from what I've seen so far, has a big interest in the freedom to use laetrile as a therapeutic option. The aim is to provide a variety of pertinent and up-to-date information in the health field.

Whether the publications discussed here are professional- or consumer-produced, they all have the common goal of featuring the things that people with special interests can directly identify with or profit from. They can be used in group discussions, made available in counseling sessions, or handed out to each new intake client. Because special-interest publications are filling the information gaps so widely decried by their respective audiences, we can expect the importance and impact of these publications to grow. Regardless of their particular philosophical stance, there are people who need them, will identify with them, and use them. Although the therapeutic journalistic concept in this book prefers to look at "needs" and "strengths" rather than "problems" and "faults" of systems, many people prefer to take an "anti" stance. There are those, for example, who would rather be antiabortion than prolife. Some would rather protest a war than demonstrate for peace. Some would rather fight disease than promote health.

A frequent characteristic of "anti" people is that they distrust and see as adverse that which lies outside of themselves. While doubting and questioning are healthy, a frequent result of the shared negativism of "anti" people is an exaggeration of the aspect that binds them together. For example, cancer victims who are fighting against existing services and treatments are using and emphasizing the "sick" part of themselves to the possible exclusion of some of their "normal" attributes. They may be dwelling on their disability and their unpleasant experiences with established treatment practices to the point where they not only ascribe malevolence to current treatments but will trust their care in no other hands but their own. Not seeing the forest through the trees, they become *exclusive*.

In contrast, the "pros" tend to try to work from within to create better systems. They too see shortcomings in what is presently available but realize they don't possess all the necessary professional expertise to change things themselves. Rather than take matters into their own hands they usually try to arrange communication interchanges with those who have expertise and are more experienced. They are *inclusive*.

This philosophical meandering is included for the sole purpose of helping you realize some of your underlying assumptions about the care people are receiving in your realm of therapeutic interest. To be aware of your views is to make the most of them. Regardless of your particular stance, realize that it *will* show in your publication, as will the philosophies of your contributors. If you go against the grain of your readers, you will fail. If you use your insights to better understand your audience, to skillfully help them to articulate *their* needs and concerns, to adeptly match need with strength or resource, then you will succeed as a helper in the true sense of that word. The important things to remember, then, are:

(1) Get to know your readers and the services and resources available to them. Know the community. Familiarize resources and break down systemic complexities.

(2) Use your publication to bring people in *common* together with the *community* via *communication*. Awareness and interchange through communication are the overriding goals.

Remember:

Therapeutic publications can address diverse kinds of audiences and can have a number of orientations. The important thing is that they support, educate, and fill the communication and information needs of their readers.

OPTIONS FOR THE THERAPEUTIC JOURNALIST IN OTHER MEDIA

You've come this far in the development of the therapeutic journalistic concept. You've borne with me throughout the discussions of publication planning and production and have faithfully worked each excrcise. You agree with the principles and elements of therapeutic journalism, but you're not interested in newspaper publishing and couldn't afford it if you were. Or you *are* interested in publication production but still can't afford it or find anyone who can.

There are many tributaries and streams running off from the therapeutic journalistic "rio grande." "Like what?," you ask? Well. . . Do you have one or more daily newspapers in your city? A Shopping Guide that shows up in your mailbox every Wednesday? A community weekly featuring events in your own neighborhood? Do you get publications from local colleges and universities, a variety of area agencies, and nearby service organizations? Do you get a church newsletter?

Peruse these and you'll see how many could benefit from featuring some good ol' therapeutic journalism. If your special-interest group is a particularly "hidden" one—like alcoholics, battered women, and "nervous" folk—the more established and general media are the more likely ways to reach them. When you think about it, look how everyone stands to gain from therapeutic features: the papers will have some new and exciting ideas brought to them, the readers will have help come right through the front door, and you just may end up landing a job as a regular, and paid, contributor. Freelancing in as many places as you can may result in something permanent and steady. After all, reflect on just how needed you are: Foster parents, victims of sexual assaults, spouses of the terminally ill—all community-based special-interest groups—have no better means to get in touch with common others. Institution-based special-interest groups similarly can be reached through therapeutic features in their facility's publication. Student special-interest groups, and their families, could be brought together through therapeutic articles in their school's newsletter and student publications.

Perhaps existing agency publications could benefit from some changes. You could sell your therapeutic journalistic skills to agencies who want advice on how to strengthen their communication efforts. You could become one agency's new editor or a group of agencies' consultant. To offset possible new costs, you could recommend such things as a change to a bimonthly or quarterly schedule, consolidation of communication programs, or changes in the distribution system.

The creative outlets for therapeutic journalistic article writers are seemingly endless. If you prefer talking to writing, there are opportunities for the therapeutic journalist in radio and television as well. These would even be preferred media for those of you interested in helping people with visual impairments. Your local broadcast media—public and cable television, community and college radio stations, and institutional closed-circuit TV programs—would all be likely candidates for new and refreshing ideas in the area of therapeutic journalism. And many may be very open to hearing your suggestions. Some also may be looking for some good local talent to nurture and promote. Here too it may be possible to land a job as a talk show host or other regular attraction.

To combine your interests in broadcast and print media, consider doing features for the television and radio papers, supplements, and columns. One idea would be to pull together all of the broadcasts affecting a particular special-interest group and write a feature that tells, sells, and connects. Here is an example: I've noticed a number of movies and made-for-TV specials lately on the divorced man, his problems, resources, and trial-and-error coping strategies. Newly divorced men may receive some comfort and empathy from these programs. They may receive helpful advice from shows featuring one-dish meals or shoestring budgeting. They may like hearing that some of their favorite professional ballplayers are also renewed bachelors. They might be interested in exercise and getting-back-into-shape programs. Attention can be brought to those programs that feature local activities and nite spots. A feature could be: "Bachelor again. How they made it, how you can."

A therapeutic journalist is a therapeutic journalist regardless of media or money. The concept can be taken everywhere. It can be helpful to anyone. None of the ideas mentioned in this section requires a financial outlay of any kind and all of the media could benefit from sponsoring features of the type discussed throughout this book. Ideas for messages have been discussed. You can pick and choose among the media.

However, you still have a little work to do: Finish this book and do or redo all the exercises, especially those on special interest group characterization, goal definition, and feature and resource identification. With all of this behind you, there's nothing in the line of therapeutic journalism that you can't do.

Finally:

Remember that a therapeutic journalist doesn't just look at one medium to the exclusion of others. In fact, a therapeutic journalist realizes that all of our media resources must be simultaneously involved in the goals we have set for ourselves. Therapeutic journalism is, after all, a concept for everyone's use and benefit. The more people we can reach more of the time, the more help we can be.

Appendix: Some Client-Oriented Publications

Title	Publisher	Cost
The Independent	Published quarterly by: Center for Independent Living, Inc. 2539 Telegraph Avenue Berkeley, CA 94104 Editor: Vicki Lewis	By subscription, $4 per year
The Independent Observer	The Independent Observer 121 Squire Hall SUNY Buffalo Buffalo, NY 14214	Write for current subscription information

Madness Network News	Published quarterly by: Madness Network News, Inc. P.O. Box 684 San Francisco, CA 94101 Contact: Tanya Temkin	Free to psychiatric inmates, $1 for prisoners, $5 to other individuals. individuals. Back issues available from $.50 to $.75
Constructive Action for Good Health Magazine	**Published Monthly by:** **B 1104 Ross Towers** 710 Lodi Street Syracuse, NY 13203 Editor: Shirley Burghard	By subscription, **$6 per year**
The AA Grapevine	Published monthly by: The AA Grapevine, Inc. 468 Park Avenue, South New York, NY 10016 Editor: anonymous	By subscription, $5 per year. Single copies, $.50
NSAC Newsletter	Published monthly by: NSAC Newsletter **1234 Massachusetts** Avenue, N.W. Washington, DC 20005 Editor: David Park	Write for current subscription inforation
Paraplegia Life	**Published Quarterly by:** **National Spinal Cord Injury** **Foundation** **Central Business Office** **369 Elliott Street** Newton, Upper Falls, MA 02164 Editorial Office: 505 North Lake Shore Drive Chicago, IL 60611 Editor: Jim Smittkamp	By subscription, $6 per year for non-members. Members receive automatic sub-scriptions

The GREEN SourceBook	Published annually by: SourceBook Publications, Inc. P.O. Box 1586 Winter Park, FL 32789 Managing Editor: John M. Erving, Jr.	By subscription $15 per year. Includes Green Papers
MMC Focus on Health	Published regularly by: Metropolitan Medical Center 900 South Eighth Street Minneapolis, MN 55404 Editor: Candy Johnson	None
Outreach	Published quarterly by: Communications and Public Affairs The Ohio State University Hospitals Starling Loving Hall Columbus, OH 43210 Editor: Jan Tremaine	None
News	Published regularly by: New York State Office for the Aging Agency Building 2 Empire State Plaza Albany, NY 12223 Editor: Richard Wendover	None
Health Law Newsletter	Published monthly by: National Health Law Program 2401 Main Street Santa Monica, CA 90405 Editor: Geoffrey Brown	None
Self-Help Reporter	Published regularly by: National Self-Help Clearinghouse 33 West 42nd Street New York, NY 10036 Editor: Audrey Gartner	None

Institutions, Etc.

Published monthly by:
Institutions, Etc.
Room 1024, Dupont Circle
Bldg.
1346 Connecticut Avenue, N.W.
Washington, DC 20036
Editor: Jerome G. Miller

Individual rate,
$22/yr, student
$15/yr. Resident of
institution or
alternative, $2/yr.

The Choice

Published quarterly by:
The Choice
146 Main Street
Suite 408
Los Altos, CA 94022
Editor: Michael L. Culbert

By subscription,
$12 per year

8

EVALUATING THERAPEUTIC JOURNALISTIC EFFORTS

A Crash Course

Evaluation principles and survey examples are presented for your consideration and use.

THE BOTTOM LINE TO ANY endeavor is, "Has what you've done made any difference? How do you know?"

Evaluation is what we do when we want to see if we're meeting our objectives (Exercise 5), when we want to discover the particular strengths and weaknesses of our efforts, and when we want to find out if what we're doing is worth the time, energy, and money we're spending to do it. *Evaluation* is what we do when we're told to demonstrate our usefulness.

This chapter will discuss an evaluation done for *TODAY*. Hopefully, it will give you ideas on what to look for, what to ask, and what to expect. Before going into *TODAY*'s surveys and their results, however, a very brief orientation to evaluation is necessary. We know it's important to discover the needs and interests of our special-interest group before embarking on a therapeutic journalistic venture or adventure. When we ask members of our potential audience what they're concerned about, confused about, or angry about, we are conducting a *needs assessment*. When we now what the needs are, we set about trying to fill them. That's when we write our goals and objectives and *plan* our therapeutic journalistic strategies. When we have plans it is logical that we *implement* them. Now *evaluation* enters the picture: We want to see if the plans and the implementation of those plans are relevant and helpful. So we begin to collect data for decision-making purposes. What we discover in evaluation will be used in further planning and implementation, which will then have to be evaluated again, and so on. What we have is a circular and continuous process we designate by the acronym PIE: P for Planning, I for implementation, and E for Evaluation. A pie is circular and so is the PIE process.

Let's focus on evaluation and explore the kinds of things we might want to study. Consider for a moment what goes into your therapeutic journalistic efforts and what you hope comes out. Think how you change inputs into outputs by operations we will call thruputs. Our inputs are what goes into the paper, broadcast, etc. Questions might be: (1) Does the paper look nice? (2) Is it readable? (3) Was the article or script well written? (4) Were the important topics selected? (5) Is the mailing list appropriate? (6) Were the resource people used knowledgeable and understandable? Thruput questions focus on product distribution and utilization. Questions here might be: (1) Who is using the product, how, and where? (2) To what extent did the feature or product support other therapeutic intervention methods? (3) To what extent is therapeutic journalism really an adjunct therapist? (4) Are my efforts used to stimulate discussion or some other form of action? (5) What processes or procedures are activitated by my efforts? (6) Are my efforts getting to the target audience? Output questions are designed to assess outcomes and results. Questions might be: (1) What differences have I made? (2) Are people being helped? (3) Is a larger number of people being appropriately referred to services? (4) Do people in my special-interest group feel less isolated and more committed to one another? (5) Do they feel less alienated, more integrated, and more independent? (6) Are they participating in the community more? (7) Is there a reduced demand on agencies for similar information?

Some of our questions are best judged by experts, some we can answer ourselves (like a publication's readability), and some are best answered directly by the consumers of our efforts. There are many evaluation methods, but when you are working with large numbers of people—as we hope we are—then some form of questionnaire seems most practical. A mass-oriented method is needed for a mass form of communication. Questionnaires can be broken down into those widely circulated by mail or other mass distribution method and those used in getting responses from a small sample through interviewing. As we shall see, *TODAY* used both. This is why: A mailed questionnaire, or one circulated in mass, is a relatively quick and economical way to reach a lot of people. Because people can only respond to what is asked of them and therefore can't offer much free comment, because the evaluator can't go back and ask people to explain their answers, and because some people just won't be bothered with questionnaires or can't understand them, a small sample of mental health clients was chosen at random for follow-up personal interviews. The sample was small because personal interviews are time-consuming and costly. To help keep the cost down, I had a doctoral student conduct the interviews. She was easy to orient and train, had a flexible enough schedule, and was pleased to do this because it gave her experience in the field. In addition, we arranged independent study credits for her work on behalf of *TODAY*. I mention all this because the same arrangements could be made between you and a student or two from your local college or university.

So *TODAY* was evaluated. The forms used are in the Appendix for your use and replication; the results will be summarized to provide you with some gauge of therapeutic journalism's acceptability and appeal. Let us now explore the driving forces that led to *TODAY's* evaluation.

Remember:
Evaluation is part of a circular or feedback process involving planning, implementation, and evaluation (PIE).

TODAY'S EVALUATION EXPERIENCES

While such responses to *TODAY* as support letters and word-of-mouth testimonies were positive, and it looked like *TODAY* was filling a useful role, a more extensive evaluation was necessary to determine whether or not its target readership was, in fact, satisfied with this resource.

Among the most frequently used methods to survey a publication's strengths and impact are responses to coupons and readership surveys. While both of these methods are certainly biased (those who choose to respond must differ in some way from those who don't), they are relatively economical, minimally disruptive to participants, reach a large section of the readership, and the results can be compared to those of other publications. Already *TODAY* had had responses to coupons that suggested that responses to a readership survey might not be as low as had been originally feared.[1] Accordingly, a return-addressed, postage-paid postcard was included in each copy of the February, 1977 issue. The press run for this issue was 3,206. The questionnaire asked for anonymous ratings of the paper's general helpfulness, the respondents' degree of familiarity with it, their current major concerns regarding mental health matters, their primary mental health service and community activities, and those aspects of the paper they liked the most and found helpful. The postcard was pretested by randomly inserting a small amount of them in an earlier issue. This postcard appears in Appendix A and is a model for you to use for the time when you may want to survey the readers of *your* therapeutic publication.

RESULTS

The frequencies of responses obtained for each question are shown in Table 8.1. One of the most interesting results was that 4.2% of the questionnaires were returned. For editorial research, this is a good return as editors generally expect roughly a 3% or 4% return. This possible indication of high acceptance of the paper was also suggested by the reported number of issues read. At least five issues had been read by 65% of the respondents. In fact the average number of issues read was twenty, which is high since only thirty-six had been published at the time of the survey. This result means that the people who chose to respond were probably the "loyal readers." This loyalty may account for the average pass along rate for *TODAY* (the number of people who are reported to read each copy) of four, which is also a high figure.

TABLE 8.1
Frequency of Responses to Questions Asked
on *TODAY* Reader Survey Postcard[1]

Please put an X next to the choices that best fit your thoughts and feelings about *TODAY*.

(1) How many issues of *TODAY* have you read, at least in part?
(9) this is my first   (20) between 2 and 5   (88) more than 5   About how many?
(20.4 mean)

(2a) Please rate *TODAY* on its helpfulness and importance to you.
(38) excellent   (63) good   (12) fair   (4) poor

(2b) What do you usually find helpful in *TODAY*? (Please check all that apply to you.)
(8) coupons
(54) tips given
(58) others' personal experiences
(77) news about places and events
(38) jokes and pictures
(92) news about mental health related issues
(26) a favorite feature(s). Which? _____
(15) other. What? _____
(6) none of it

(3) Do other people read your copies of *TODAY*? (79) yes (30) no.
How many people? (4 mean)

(4) What are you doing now? (Please check all that apply to you.)
(20) living alone in the community
(52) living with friends, spouse, or family
(9) living in a supervised place
(6) in incare
(8) in daycare or outcare
(45) working
(18) unemployed
(71) am a mental health or related area (para) professional

(5) What are your main concerns right now? (Please check only those that are very important to you right now.)
(56) family
(50) friends
(30) getting along in the community
(38) money
(39) job
(40) physical health
(28) having a good place to live
(19) finding things to do
(22) *getting* myself together
(35) *keeping* myself together
(38) trying new and different things for me
(29) other. What? _____

Comments and suggestions (54) _____

THANK YOU

1. Total number of respondents = 135.
Total number of postcards circulated = 3,206.
Frequencies do not add up to 135: in some cases less than because of nonresponse, in some cases more than because of multiple checking.

TODAY was rated good or excellent in helpfulness and importance by 75% of the respondents. Even those who gave *TODAY* a lower rating wrote twice as many positive as negative comments. All in all, 40% of the respondents volunteered additional positive comments about the paper.[2]

For the most part, the features seen as being most helpful are the ones given the most emphasis in *TODAY*. News about community places and events (checked by 57% of respondents) and mental health and related issues (checked by 68% of respondents) were the overwhelming favorites. Other popular features are "tips given" (40% of respondents) and "others' personal experiences" (43% of respondents). When these favorite features were cross-tabulated with the respondents' primary activity in the community or mental health system, it was found that (of those guessed to be mental health clients) those living in supervised places, and those active in daycare and outcare, liked "others' personal experiences" and the "news about mental health and related area issues." Those in daycare and outcare also reported interest in "news about community places and events," and the incare respondents liked "jokes and pictures," "news about community places and events," and a variety of miscellaneous features such as keeping up an attractive home and personal appearance, and legal and human rights. Finally, the most common major concerns were with family and friends, but all the attachments were well represented.

Because a disproportionate number of respondents to the postcard survey reported themselves as being professionals or paraprofessionals, a second survey form was designed to poll only those known to be mental health clients. It was decided that a personal interview format would be most appropriate.

THE PERSONAL INTERVIEWS

Although I designed the postcard survey, I wanted a survey form that had been "tried and tested" for the personal interviews. I found one in a doctoral dissertation (Collins, 1972) and with some modifications and adaptations had an instrument that would not only provide follow-up to the postcard survey but would supply some additional information. This form appears in Appendix B. Feel free to use, modify, or adapt it in your evaluation.

Forty-eight clients were chosen at random and were asked to volunteer for a "community survey": one that wouldn't take a lot of time, would ask for their opinions on a number of things, and would give them a chance to have input into some possible changes. *TODAY* was not mentioned at all (until halfway into the interview) so they had no idea they were going to be asked about this resource.

This form started out with a warm-up exercise: innocuous questions concerning where clients lived and for how long, and their ratings of various community "institutions" such as the police department, churches, etc. The questionnaire then surveyed their general media usage.

A potpourri of headlines were read to respondents that featured a variety of topics found in the daily print media and topics from past issues of *TODAY*. The four headlines rated the highest were all from *TODAY*: three featuring news about mental health-related issues and one about tips on applying for jobs. The ratings of the headlines were done before any clues were given that this was a survey about *TODAY*.

After the section on headlines, the interviewees were asked to focus on *TODAY* and relate something in particular they liked about it. The gamut of *TODAY* features were mentioned at least once. When respondents were asked to rate *TODAY* on appearance, content, readability, and point of view, 74% of the *TODAY* readers said it was doing a better job overall than other papers they had seen.

When read from a list of media including the area's two daily newspapers, community weeklies, college papers, and some nationals, *TODAY* received a modal rating of five, five being of highest possible interest to the interviewee.

Also, *TODAY* was rated by the respondents as being the most popular newspaper among their client friends, and the respondents themselves had read a mean of four issues of *TODAY* in the last six months (*TODAY* is a monthly publication).

The percentage of those interviewed who rated *TODAY* as being good or excellent in helpfulness and importance to them was only 59% as compared to 75% of the postcard survey respondents. (This seems to bear out the idea that a publication's mail questionnaire respondents are the most loyal and satisfied readers.) These results are not discouraging, however, since the negative respondents all rated the *TODAY* headlines very high. Three of the four "poors" even believed *TODAY* "does a better job overall than other papers they have seen!" Perhaps these people were just not indulgers in the media.

Other interesting results of this survey are: (1) 78% of the *TODAY* readers have regular access to it; (2) the vast majority of respondents are living in the community and are concerned mainly with "family," "friends," and "keeping themselves together" (this correlates with the postcard survey finding on client concerns); (3) 67% of the respondents have told others about their mental health background, 1/3 of them have then been "treated differently" as a result of this, and, of the latter, 44% don't like the special treatment they have received.

In Conclusion:
(1) The results of two survey efforts attest to the value, helpfulness, and importance of *TODAY*.
(2) Respondents to the surveys reported strong interests in features that are designed to promote community participation and awareness and self-development. More of these features should be planned and included.
(3) Responses to the surveys indicate a favorable tendency for communication via this vehicle to be seen as helpful and useful. In this respect *TODAY* appears to be bridging some information and communication gaps that exist between and among impacting systems.
(4) Further documentation of *TODAY*'s functional utility needs to be conducted. Yet the reponses at this juncture indicate there is value in and need for resources such as *TODAY*. Therefore, duplication and replication efforts of this therapeutic publication are likely to be worthwhile.

(5) As for methodology, the results of the two surveys were so similar that one probably need only use the more economical postcard format. However, it should be taken into account that positive results to postcard surveys are somewhat inflated, as it is a publication's loyal readers who tend to follow through on this survey method.

EXERCISE 13

EVALUATION NOTES

While you are planning an evaluation strategy, the most important things to keep in mind are:

What Do I Want to Find Out?	Who Can Tell Me?	How Can I Ask Them?
1.	1.	1.
2.	2.	2.
3.	3.	3.
4.	4.	4.
5.	5.	5.
6.	6.	6.
7.	7.	7.
8.	8.	8.
9.	9.	9.
10.	10.	10.

Once you have some therapeutic journalistic efforts underway and have done some research on evaluation, you may want to survey your audience. Exercise 13 will be helpful to you then much more so than now. Therefore, you can file it away for future use.

NOTES

1. A coupon was run in *TODAY* featuring a free diabetic cookbook while a simultaneous news release was printed in the largest local daily. The response from *TODAY* far surpassed that from the daily, as reported to me by the local American Diabetes Association chapter.

At another time, the local health department offered a free "quit smoking kit" through: (a) a *TODAY* coupon, (b) releases in three local weeklies, (c) a large area daily, and (d) radio and TV spots. Here, *TODAY* provided the largest single source of requests for the free kit. Results like these attract advertisers! Try to get them.

2. There was one outstanding suggestion for improvement that I recommend you consider: to run a box score of how local legislators and other local policy-makers vote on legislation affecting your readers. You may want to have an entire column on legislative bills and their sponsors and advocates.

REFERENCE

COLLINS, E. L. (1972) "The standardized community survey for newspapers: a standardized, low-cost, systematic and objective method for newspapers to obtain information about themselves and their communities." Doctoral dissertation, Syracuse University.

SUGGESTED EVALUATION RESOURCES

FERMAN, L. A. (1969) "Some perspectives on evaluating social welfare programs." Annals of the American Academy of Political and Social Sciences (September).
ROSSI, P. H. and W. WILLIAMS (1972) Evaluating Social Programs. New York: Seminar Press.
TRIPODI, T., P. FELLIN, and E. EPSTEIN (1971) Social Program Evaluation. Itasca, IL: Peacock.

9

MEDIA AND THERAPY

Growing Together

A few final points as we prepare to go our separate therapeutic journalistic ways.

BEFORE READING THIS BOOK our most common views of therapeutic media were poetry-writing workshops, creative writing workshops, and a variety of art and music therapy efforts. All of these programs are geared toward improved self-expression—trying to use paper, canvas, or tone to express, vent, and communicate those aspects of ourselves we can only release indirectly and through a socially sanctioned symbol of creative expression. Albeit therapeutic, these media do not allow for the things advocated in the preceding seven chapters: reattachment to external systems, community integration, and communication interaction and exchange on a variety of levels with a multitude of systems.

It is hoped that the reader of this book has been sold on therapeutic journalism as a concept and as the producer of products that are needed, that have a certain amount of built-in acceptance, and that are helpful and useful to everyone concerned. What but media can so effectively intervene in poor communications, miscommunications, and communication voids. The media have been drafted into therapeutic service.

Our audiences will interact with a multitude of systems on a number of different communication levels. The reciprocity of the interactions and interchanges, the transactional emphasis, means we may have some influence on the accommodation of systems to our common needs and wants. In our complex time, in this age of anxiety, outer disconnectedness, inner desperation, we can do something to help shape, organize, and structure all that we are and have around us into a total personal sanctum that gives us a sense of responsibility yet liberation, a sense of control and independence; a sense of well-being and personal satisfaction, a feeling of belonging and meaning. With our self-awareness and self-fulfillment we work toward integrating that self with others. Self-reliance becomes a strength only when the self can recognize and use what it needs from its milieu to maintain balance and attachment. We gather the parts of that fragmented milieu into a concise guidebook of options to be used in building a meaningful sense of self and well-being. It is the nature of people to be attached, to be complete, to have a sense of meaning. They will get it somehow whether it be by adaptive or maladaptive means. We provide the information stimuli to help them choose the former or replace the latter with a more healthful or "normal" lifestyle.

These goals are arduous enough. Altogether they seem a formidable task. Yet this book has given you ideas, in much more concrete terms than I've used here, on how to make *all* of the above work for you, your special-interest group, and your community. From here on out, it's up to you to carry the ball. You choose your special-interest group (there are and are always likely to be hundreds out there who need you: mastectomy patients, parents in crisis, people in grief, ex-addicts, ex-inmates, as well as the special-interest groups already mentioned). It's up to you to talk with them, discover what they need and want to know, start their sharing and comparing, support them in their reattaching and balancing. If you want to do it, you can do it. If you can do it, you will do it.

You'll work hard. You'll have people tell you that you gave them a new idea, new hope; you'll have people call your paper a rag. You'll be read with fervor; you'll be ignored. You'll be lauded; you'll be sharply criticized. You'll be seen as a professional; you'll be called incompetent. But you are *doing something*. Wilbur Schramm (1971) has a fitting analogy for the therapeutic journalist: Reread this every time you wonder why in hell you ever decided to be a therapeutic journalist; reread it every time you need to feel humble:

> I know a baker in southern Asia who gets up at dawn every morning to bake goods for sale. He can't force them on anyone . . . all he can do is display his wares. He chooses a place where he knows crowds will pass. He bakes things of a kind he has found many people like. He tries to display them attractively. Then it is up to the patrons. The crowds move past. Some passersby will see the cakes and breads; some will not. Some will be hungry and looking for food; others not. Some will be looking specifically for cakes or bread; others not. Some, because they have bought good wares from this specific baker in the past, will be looking for his stand especially; others, not. Some will see the cakes, find their appetites stimulated, and reach in their pockets for coins; and they may or may not find any. And if they buy, they may or may not eat any or all of what they buy; they may or may not eat it with jam; they may or may not taste it and throw it away [Schramm and Roberts, 1971: 16].

REFERENCE

SCHRAMM, W. and D. ROBERTS [Eds.] (1971) The Process and Effects of Mass Communication. Urbana: University of Illinois Press.

Please, everyone...

We want all of us to have a better "TODAY" -- a paper that is more in line with all of our concerns and interests. To do this we need your help. We've attached a postcard to this page in every copy of "TODAY" so you can tell us what you already read and what your main concerns are. We'll continue featuring only those things you enjoy and will add features centered around your areas of special interest.

Please fill out and mail the postcard attached to this page -- even if you got one of the samples last month. It'll only take you a few minutes. And, no postage stamp is necessary.

If you have any questions, please phone us at 886-1242 or write to us at: Mental Health Association of Erie County, Inc., 366 Forest Avenue, Buffalo, NY 14213.

We can only better "TODAY" with your help. Now's your chance to have more of a say in what this paper is about.

Please fill out the below, tear off, and mail
(no postage necessary)

- -

Please put an X next to the choices that best fit your thoughts and feelings about "TODAY"

1) How many issues of "TODAY" have you read, at least in part?
    ___ this is my first   ___ between 2 and 5   ___ more than 5. About how many? ___

2a) Please rate "TODAY" on its helpfulness and importance to you.
    ___ excellent   ___ good   ___ fair   ___ poor

2b) What do you usually find helpful in "TODAY?" (Please check all that apply to you.)
    ___ coupons   ___ news about mental health related issues
    ___ tips given   ___ a favorite feature(s). Which? _____
    ___ others' personal experiences
    ___ news about places and events ___ other. What? _____
    ___ jokes and pictures   ___ none of it

3) Do other people read your copies of "TODAY?" ___ yes ___ no. How many people? ___

4) What are you doing now? (Please check all that apply to you.)
    ___ living alone in the community   ___ in daycare or outcare
    ___ living with friends, spouse, or family ___ working
    ___ living in a supervised place   ___ unemployed
        the community   ___ am a mental health or related
    ___ in incare   area (para)professional

5) What are your main concerns right now? (please check only those that are very
    important to you right now.)
    ___ family   ___ having a good place to live
    ___ friends   ___ finding things to do
    ___ getting along in the community ___ getting myself together
    ___ money   ___ keeping myself together
    ___ job   ___ trying new and different things for me
    ___ physical health   ___ other. What? _____

Comments and suggestions _____

THANK YOU

FIRST CLASS
PERMIT NO. 8875
BUFFALO, NY

BUSINESS REPLY MAIL
NO POSTAGE STAMP NECESSARY IF MAILED IN THE UNITED STATES

POSTAGE WILL BE PAID BY

MENTAL HEALTH ASSOCIATION OF ERIE COUNTY, INC.

366 FOREST AVENUE

BUFFALO, NY 14213

1 G 1 77

A P P E N D I X B:
T O D A Y'S P E R S O N A L
I N T E R V I E W I N G F O R M

FREQUENCIES AND MEANS[1] FROM
TODAY SURVEY II
COMMUNITY AND LIVING CONDITIONS
(preface with introduction)

1. First, I'd like to know what city, town, or village you live in. <u>(Buffalo area = 46)</u>

2. How long have you lived in this city, town, or village or within 10 miles
   of it?

   <u> (18.9 years = mean)</u>

3. What is your overall rating of this community as a place to live -- excellent,
   good, fair, or poor?

   <u>(5)</u> excellent   <u>(29)</u> good   <u>(11)</u> fair   <u>(3)</u> poor

4. In every community, the schools, the newspapers, the government, and other
   organizations -- each has a different job to do. I'd like to know how you feel
   about the ones around here.

   I'll read seven major categories of organizations. Please give each one a
   score from zero to 5 depending on how good a job you think it's doing. If
   it's doing the worst possible job, give it a score of zero. If it's doing a
   perfect job, give it a score of 5. Otherwise, give it any score from zero
   to 5 that expresses how you feel about the kind of job it's doing. Now,
   what's your rating of the job being done around here by:
   (Mean:)
   <u>(3.4)</u> the public schools?

   <u>(3.6)</u> the newspapers?

   <u>(4.0)</u> the radio stations?

   <u>(3.6)</u> the television stations?

   <u>(2.8)</u> the local government?

   <u>(3.7)</u> the churches?

   <u>(3.5)</u> the police department?

   <u>(3.3)</u> the mental health department?

   <u>(3.6)</u> the hospitals?

   <u>(3.7)</u> the mental health facilities?

[1]Total number of respondents = 48

GENERAL COMMUNICATION USAGE

5. How many different newspapers, and magazines, do you see regularly at
   the present time?   <u>(4 = Mean)</u>

6. In most communities, there's one radio station or one newspaper or one
   television station which a person can use to keep up with information about
   his or her major interests.

From which one particular source do you yourself get the most information
about what's important to you:

(20) A particular radio station? which? _____

(10) A particular newspaper? which? _____

(14) A particular TV station? which? _____

 (4) Friends or other sources?

7. If you had some important news you wanted people to know about, which one
    particular radio station or newspaper or TV station or other organization
    would you give it to, to spread that information?

    (Wide variety) _____

NEWSPAPERS

8. I'm going to read the names of some papers which come into this community.
    I'd like to know how interesting each of these papers is to you personnally.
    To rate each one, please think of a score from zero to 5. If a paper is not
    at all interesting to you, give it a score of zero. If a paper has the
    highest possible interest to you, give it a score of 5. Otherwise, give it
    any score between zero and 5 that best expresses your degree of interest in it.

    Now, what's your rating of:
    (Mean:)
    (4.0) Buffalo Evening News?

    (3.7) Buffalo Courier Express?

    (3.6) TODAY...Your Mental Health in Your Community?

    (4.0) New York Times?

    (3.4) National Enquirer?

    (3.1) Local college papers?

    Lastly, _____A community newspaper. For example, The Cheektowaga Times,
    Kensington Topics, The Challenger, The West Side Times, and so on.

    (3.5) _____

9. I'll read the list of papers again and this time I'd like to know approxi-
    mately how many issues of each you've read in the past six months. You
    don't have to be exact, just give me your best guess. Ready? okay....
    (Mean:)
    (74.4)Buffalo Evening News

    (55.1)Buffalo Courier Express

     (4.4)TODAY...Your Mental Health in Your Community

     (7.7)New York Times

    (10.8)National Enquirer

    (10.2)Local college papers

    (14.6)community newspaper _____

10. I'm going to read the list of papers one more time and now I'd like to know
    your best guess of how many people around here, not including the staff though,
    read each of the papers. Ready? okay....
    (Mean:)
    (94.1)Buffalo Evening News

(104.8)Buffalo Courier Express

(189.7)TODAY....Your Mental Health in Your Community

(115.1)New York Times

(125.3)National Enquirer

(158.8)Local college papers

(121.2)community newspaper _____

11. Are there, any other papers, other than those mentioned, that you read regularly?

_____

_____

12. Now imagine that, for the next year, you could see only one paper regularly, no others. Which one paper would you want?

    (3 said "TODAY")   (42 said a variety of others)

Why did you pick this particular one?

    (34 said "Quality Content")   (11 said "It's Available")

13. Now I'd like to know how interested you might be in reading different kinds of newspaper articles and features. I'll read some headlines and titles. After I read each one, please give me your score between zero and 5, zero being of no interest to you, 5 being of major interest to you. Give it any score beween zero and 5 that best expresses how likely you would be to read the item if it appeared in a newspaper. (Means:)

Unemployment is at its highest level in 8 years. (3.8)

How to pick a good therapist. (4.0)

Amherst proposes to build a $4 million junior high school. (3.3)

Buffalo Philharmonic to feature all Brahms-Beethoven concert.(3.8)

Narcotic probe nets five in Niagara Falls. (3.3)

The right to refuse mental health treatment. (4.0)

Town tax rate will increase by $15 per thousand unless budget drastically cut. (3.9)

Tips on applying for a job. (4.4)

Ways to manage your money more wisely. (4.0)

Sex education pilot program begins in public schools. (4.0)

Fire destroys large industry; hundreds out of work. (3.7)

Cause for schizophrenia found. (3.9)

Ideas for a healthy diet. (3.6)

GOP, DEMS in close race for control of mayoral seat. (3.4)

Little League all-stars in world series. (3.2)

Three Buffalo men injured in auto mishap.(2.9)

Woman elected board president. (3.3)

Don't mix tranquilizers with vitamin F4. (4.1)

14. Now I'd like to know if there is anything about the newspaper "TODAY....Your Mental Health in Your Community" that you particularly like. If so, what?
    (if never seen, go to question 20)

    (12 = content)   (10 = area happenings)   (3 = tips given)

    (3 = jokes and pictures)   (6 = favorite feature)

15. Is there anything you particularly dislike about the TODAY newspaper? What?

    (6 = content)

    (1 = level)

16. I'd like to get your impressions of the TODAY newspaper even though you may not read it regularly. Therefore, if you have ever read even a single issue of TODAY, please answer either yes or no, to the questions I'll now read. In your opinion, does TODAY usually....

	yes	no
...use print that is easy to read?	(31)	(1)
...actively seek out and print all the important issues you're concerned about?	(19)	(11)
...contain enough things that interest you personally?	(26)	(6)
...report the facts accurately in its articles?	(26)	(6)
...give fair treatment to all kinds of people, regardless of their race, religion, money, age, etc.	(27)	(5)
...give fair treatment to all sides of major issues?	(20)	(10)
...keep its readers well informed on the way local systems operate?	(24)	(8)
...use clear, understandable writing?	(28)	(4)
...put the interests of the whole community and citizens ahead of its own interests?	(19)	(11)
...do a better job, overall, than other papers you have seen?	(23)	(8)

17. Now, how would you rate TODAY'S helpfulness and importance to you? Excellent, Good, Fair, or Poor?

    (5) excellent   (14) good   (9) fair   (4) poor

18. Do you get your own copy of TODAY regularly or have regular access to it?

    (25) yes   (7) no

19. Have you ever seen a questionnaire about TODAY before?

    (4) yes   (28) no

    If yes, when was that? _____

    Did you fill it out and mail it in? (1) yes   (3) no
    (If no) Why not? _____

PERSONAL CHARACTERISTICS

Just a few more brief questions, now, to help our survey.

20. What's the highest grade in school you've completed?

<u>(Mean = 11.8)</u>

21. What is your age? <u>(Mean = 29.5)</u> (indicate sex: <u>(26)</u> M <u>(22)</u> F)

22. Now I'm going to read a list of activities and please say yes if they apply to you and no if they don't.
(Yes:)
<u>(8)</u> I'm living alone in the community

<u>(38)</u> I'm living with friends, spouse, or family

<u>(17)</u> I'm living in a supervised place in the community

<u>(7)</u> I'm in incare

<u>(20)</u> I'm in daycare or out-care

<u>(11)</u> I'm working

<u>(27)</u> I'm unemployed

<u>(10)</u> I'm a mental health or related area paraprofessional or professional

23. Next, I'll read some common concerns people have. Please say yes if it applies to you and no if it doesn't. Ready? okay....

I'm concerned very much about:
(Yes:)
<u>(45)</u> my family

<u>(44)</u> my friends

<u>(41)</u> getting along in the community

<u>(36)</u> money

<u>(37)</u> a job

<u>(43)</u> my physical health

<u>(43)</u> having a good place to live

<u>(37)</u> finding things to do

<u>(40)</u> getting myself together

<u>(45)</u> keeping myself together

<u>(40)</u> trying new and different things

24. If you had the power to make just one change to make your own personal life happier, what change would you make?

25. Now, for my final questions.

You've said you're receiving (have you ever received?) mental health services. Have you told others about this - others who would have no way of knowing otherwise?

<u>(32)</u> yes <u>(16)</u> no

Have you experienced or do you expect to be treated differently because of your
mental health care?

___ (16 = Yes)   (23 = No) _____

In what way?   _____

How do you feel about this? ____ (21 care a great deal) _____

_____   _____

Thank you so much for talking with me.

                          (appropriate closing)

    I give permission to be interviewed for the "Community and Media Survey."
The information I provide can be used for education and research. However, I
understand my identity will be kept secret and that the information given by
me will be used without identifying me in any way as the source.

    Of my own free will I have decided to be part of this survey. I understand
that at any time I want to stop I can.

    I also realize I have the choice to be tape recorded or not during the in-
terview. This tape will be used for supervision purposes of the interviewer
only and I understand it will be kept secret. At any time I want the tape
recording to stop, I have only to ask and it will be stopped.

                              _____
                              Interviewee signature

                              _____
                              Date

    I will uphold all of the above for the person whose signature appears above.

                              _____
                              Interviewer signature

                              _____
                              Date

ABOUT THE AUTHOR

MARCIA S. JOSLYN-SCHERER is a therapeutic journalist. She has a bachelor's degree in journalism from Syracuse University and a masters degree in rehabilitation counseling from the State University of New York at Buffalo. She also holds a certificate from the Division of Community Psychiatry of SUNY Buffalo's School of Medicine.

She is Editor-in-chief of *TODAY . . . Your Mental Health in Your Community* and is the evaluator in the Evaluation and Technical Services Unit of the Social Services Training Project at the State University College at Buffalo.

In her spare time she does volunteer crisis counseling for a crisis intervention service and instructs SUNY Buffalo's sophomore medical students in patient-doctor communication skills.

COMMENTS ON *COMMUNICATION IN THE HUMAN SERVICES*

(1) The best aspects of this book were: _____

_____

_____

(2) Changes I would recommend are: _____

_____

_____

(3) Uses I've found for the book and its ideas are: _____

_____

_____

(4) I would be interested in receiving information about a workshop on this subject:

Name _____

Address _____

City _____ State _____ Zip _____

Phone _____ – _____

Return to: SAGE PUBLICATIONS, INC.
275 South Beverly Drive
Beverly Hills, CA 90212

DATE DUE

GAYLORD			PRINTED IN U.S.A.